# Babies At Work

## Bringing New Life to the Workplace

Carla Moquin
Parenting in the Workplace Institute

Additional copies of this book can be purchased at
www.BabiesAtWork.org
or
www.ParentingAtWork.org


If this book has any printing quality problems,
please go to www.Lulu.com for a replacement copy.

ISBN 978-0-6152-4146-3

# Notes

## References and Other Resources

This book is also available as an ebook from the Babies in the Workplace (www.BabiesAtWork.org) site, which is available for free to anyone who has bought a copy of this book. The ebook contains numerous text links to other resources and documentation for statements made in this book as well as color pictures of babies at work. For specific questions about resources or to receive your free copy of the ebook, contact Carla Moquin at carla@babiesatwork.org or (801) 897-8702.

## Clarification of Discussed Parenting Principles

There is still controversy over whether parents should co-sleep with their babies. Just as with breastfeeding (or several other suggestions made in this book), each individual parent should try different child-raising techniques to find those that work best for them and their families. But there is extensive evidence to suggest that, if you keep your baby close during sleep, breastfeed on your baby's timetable, hold your baby frequently, and use other techniques described in this book, there are many benefits to be gained. These parenting methods are completely natural and healthy for babies and are likely to lead to highly content children. But they are not the only ways to raise happy, contented babies.

## Qualifications About Quotes and Companies

The interviews for this book took place during a span covering more than two years. In a few cases, the people who previously approved quotes for this book have moved to different companies from those they worked in at the time of the interviews. I nonetheless used several of these quotes since people's employment situations are so fluid in our current world (making the book potentially outdated the day after publication if it were to contain *only* quotes from people currently employed at the same company) and since their statements still accurately describe the dynamics of the baby-friendly companies.

Dedicated to Alpha, Peri, and Echo

# Acknowledgments

I thank the companies and individuals who gave me their time and trust in sharing their experiences with (and ideas on) parenting in the workplace. I also thank the researchers, activists, and supporters who helped me in innumerable ways to reach this point. This work would not be possible without your willingness to experiment and your dedication to creating a more human-friendly workplace and a more child-friendly world.

I thank the countless friends and acquaintances who offered me encouragement in this work, shared their personal experiences, offered ideas, and, in many cases, offered me their skepticism—which continually encouraged me to learn more and strive to become the best possible advocate I can be for parenting in the workplace.

I thank my father for his invaluable help in getting this book (and my websites) designed, edited, and done on schedule, for his amazing creative and design skills, for *always* being there when I needed a new idea or a new direction, and for not hesitating to tell me when he believes there is a better way to do something. I thank Tawni J. Anderson for her constant friendship, her incredible editing abilities, her unending support and help with my efforts in this field, and for always knowing just what to say. I thank my mother for her constant support of me in everything I do. I thank Debra Lampasona for being a wonderful, integral person in my children's lives and for providing me with valuable feedback on the ideas in this book.

I thank William Charlie Miller-Moquin for being a fantastic father and friend, for his invaluable ideas and information to help with this work in continuation of his long-standing dedication to helping women achieve equality in the professional world, and for sharing in this journey.

I thank my daughters for being who they are. *None* of this would have been possible without them and I look forward to spending the rest of my life helping them to find true happiness and showing them how much they mean to me.

# Table of Contents

# PREFACE

I am a working mother, am raising two daughters, and have been amicably divorced since 2006. I worked full time as a legal secretary until the day my older child was born, returned to work for twenty hours a week when she was four weeks old, and went back to full-time work when she was five months old. After my younger child was born in 2005, I returned to full-time work when she was four weeks old and have since worked essentially full time out of financial necessity. I was unfortunately never in a position to take my children to work with me when they were babies.

One day in 2005, while looking for topics on which to write freelance articles to supplement my income, I came across a news article about a credit union that regularly allowed babies to come to work with their parents until they were six months old. When I called the company to get more information, they mentioned another company with a similar policy (this one allowed babies until eight months of age). Having had to return to work so soon after my own children's births, the concept intrigued me. I searched for more companies that allowed babies at work. After hundreds of hours of research, I was able to locate more than one hundred organizations with active babies-at-work programs.

Over the following months, I interviewed executives, managers, coworkers, and parents about babies in the workplace—and I realized that I was hearing the same comments again and again. In virtually every company, many people feared the worst before the baby program was implemented—they expected that the babies would scream all the time or that people would spend all their time playing with the babies instead of working. But in every organization with clear ground rules for parents and coworkers, this skepticism gave way to enthusiastic support once people saw how well these programs worked in practice. Babies at work were almost always highly content. The benefits for the businesses were consistent and extensive. Perhaps most notably, it cost almost nothing for the businesses to allow babies at work. Parents maintained responsibility for their babies' care (in some cases signing legal waiver forms) and provided all of the equipment; all the company had to do was establish clear rules and, perhaps, install diaper-changing tables in the restrooms.

I read every article I could find about individual companies allowing babies at work and soon realized that, as a trend, parenting in the workplace was virtually unknown. No one, not even the people in baby-friendly companies, seemed to be aware of the wide range of other companies that had successfully allowed babies at work, much less the seemingly-universal business benefits provided by well-structured programs. In June 2007, I created a website, Babies in the Workplace (www.BabiesAtWork.org), based on my research. The public interest in the site led me, in December 2007, to found a non-profit, the Parenting in the Workplace Institute. The Institute's mission is to provide education and resources for the successful implementation of babies-at-work programs and programs involving school-age children in the workplace (toddlers create a higher level of complexity for most workplaces than we currently know how to effectively handle with a template parenting-at-work program; on-site daycare currently appears to be the most appropriate child-friendly alternative for companies to offer for this age group).

This book is designed to present the growing evidence that, in many cases, the routine segregation of children from adult society is no longer necessary and that integrating babies (and older children) into the workplace actually leads to a more holistic work environment and a healthier society.

Thank you for joining me on this journey.

August 1, 2008
Carla Moquin

# 1

# **A POSSIBLE FUTURE**

You're at the grocery store with your two children and you ask a salesperson to help you find an item—and then you realize that her baby is calmly staring at you from a comfy perch in a sling worn by his mother. When you smile at the sight of the happy child, his face lights up and he immediately smiles back, giving you an instant feeling of contentment. Feeling unexpectedly energized, you walk past a man restocking shelves while his daughter sleeps peacefully in a front pack. When you stop at the bookstore on your way home, the cashier's baby watches you intently from a swing next to the register. Your own daughter is thrilled and spends several minutes making silly faces at the baby to make him laugh. When you return home, you call to order a present for a friend's birthday, and in the background you can faintly hear the cooing of babies.

The next morning, your family gets ready for the day. As your daughter heads to school on her bicycle, you leave for work with your three-month-old son. You're off to spend the day being a parent and a professional at the same time, and you wonder what new milestone you'll watch your baby reach today while he learns about your world.

This scene could easily be reality in less than a decade. More than 100 organizations already allow parents to bring their babies to work with them every day for the first several months of life and to care for the babies while they do their jobs. These programs have involved more than 1,300 babies to date, with some companies seeing more than 50 babies come to work in recent years. These companies have discovered that parenting in the workplace is feasible and offers extensive business benefits when carefully structured. These benefits include:

- Enabling new parents to return to work earlier (if they so choose)
- Lowering employee turnover, especially among women
- Improving morale
- Increasing long-term productivity
- Enhancing teamwork and collaboration
- Lowering health care costs
- Recruiting new employees
- Attracting new customers
- Inspiring increased loyalty among existing customers

These benefits come with only nominal costs to the organization.

These programs provide extensive benefits for families, such as:

- Promoting parent-baby bonding
- Enabling breastfeeding
- Lowering feelings of isolation and role conflict for new mothers

- Reducing obstacles for professional women's advancement
- Enhancing fathers' involvement with their babies
- Increasing financial stability
- Lowering daycare costs

Babies successfully come to work in organizations in more than 30 states (and a few in other countries) and include credit unions and law firms, retail stores and consulting firms, non-profits and government agencies, and many other kinds of organizations. These programs have been successful in companies with only a few employees as well as ones with more than 3,000. These work babies are overwhelmingly content—for reasons that could transform our culture's perspective on what is "normal" baby behavior.

The concept of working alongside children is actually nothing new. For most of human history, the norm was (and still is in some cultures today) to care for children while simultaneously working to support one's family and community. In indigenous cultures, children are active participants in their society and become motivated to contribute to the community's well-being. Adults in these cultures view child-rearing as a community effort and feel invested in the development of these children with whom they interact on a daily basis.

However, since the Industrial Revolution our society has become fragmented. Many adults have minimal exposure to or experience with children until they have a baby of their own, and many new parents find themselves isolated in the early months of their babies' lives when they most need social interaction, support, and guidance. Millions of young children are segregated into artificially-structured environments at a time when they are learning faster than they will during the rest of their lives—thus missing valuable opportunities to observe and absorb the complex dynamics and nuances of human society.

Bringing babies to work bridges many of these divisions. These programs expose people to babies before they have their own children, providing them with knowledge and experience—and, thus, confidence—about parenting. New parents benefit from the social network of the workplace. Babies become part of the workplace community and they thrive on the social interaction and affection they receive. Having babies in a work environment even creates a "community parenting" atmosphere in which coworkers (even some who were initially skeptical of the idea) frequently bond with and feel invested in nurturing the children in their midst and assisting the babies' parents.

Babies cry to communicate a need; our job as adults is to meet that need as quickly as possible so that babies can return to their goal of observing and learning about their world. Babies cry only for seconds at a time—and never develop colic—in cultures in which they have extensive physical contact (and sleep with their parents instead of alone), they have their needs met within seconds and are breastfed frequently, and they are in a position to easily observe and interact with other people. The complete lack of colic in some cultures means that colic is *not* an innate biological quality of certain babies or that some babies just "want to cry."

There are babies in our society who are raised with the same care practices as in indigenous cultures but who still cry for prolonged periods—in these cases there is invariably a reason for the crying (be it physical pain, allergies, heightened sensitivity to stimulation, or other issues). The real keys for parents are to understand that babies *always* cry for a reason, even if it may sometimes take time to figure it out, and that healthy babies who are cared for in the ways described in this book are far more likely to cry only minimally and be highly content with their world.

For parents whose babies are colicky, the critical factor is giving the babies lots of physical contact and emotional support while you're trying to figure out the source of the problem. Even for a very unhappy baby, feeling safe and secure close to a person can make all the difference in how the baby views his situation. There is *no* benefit for a baby from being left alone to cry. (However, if you are the parent of a colicky baby and you are feeling emotionally overwhelmed such that you are tempted to shake or hurt your baby in any way, find someone else to hold the baby for a bit or put the baby down and take a few moments out of the room until you feel more stabilized.) Ideas and resources for helping babies with colic are in the Keeping Babies Happy chapter.

It turns out that the dynamics of structured babies-at-work programs mirror many of the patterns in indigenous cultures in which colic doesn't exist: babies at work often spend a lot of time in carriers or on parents' laps, they are often breastfed, they receive extensive social interaction, and parents usually respond very quickly to their cries to avoid disturbing coworkers. These practices are ideal for raising highly social, healthy, and well-adjusted children, and the presence of these happy babies invariably causes a profound transformation of the traditional office atmosphere—and could cause a revolution in how we view the integration of work and family.

| 10 | Top Ten Tips for A Successful Baby Program |
|----|---------------------------------------------|
|    | Parents Sign Liability Form                 |

# 2

# CONVERTED SKEPTICS

> I just couldn't see it working. But they sold
> me on [the program], and I've been really
> happy with it.
>> Fran Oswald, Branch Manager
>> Schools Financial Credit Union

## Skeptics

Nearly all of the executives and managers from the businesses with babies-at-work programs, as well as many of the parents who participated with their babies, were initially highly skeptical that bringing babies to work could work. Since many in our society believe that babies are "supposed" to cry regularly and for long periods of time, many people in these businesses naturally assumed that it would be impossible to get much work done with babies around. Fran Oswald, a branch manager at Schools Financial Credit Union, admitted:

> When they first announced it—when it went
> live—I was thinking, "That's ridiculous.
> How do they expect me to run a branch with
> babies?" I just couldn't see it working. But

they sold me on [the program], and I've been really happy with it.

Susan Matthews of Borshoff, a public relations firm, also said that her company had some skeptics: "People were worrying about the baby screaming or whether they would be able to get work done. But it became a joy for everyone."

Brian Moline was an attorney at the Kansas Insurance Department when they first began their baby program under the direction of then-Commissioner Kathleen Sebelius (Ms. Sebelius went on to become the governor of Kansas). He admits that he was initially very resistant to the idea of bringing babies into the workplace. He was concerned about public perceptions regarding babies coming to work in a governmental agency. He was also worried about liability issues and wondered if people would be able to get any work done with a baby around.

Most of these companies felt as though they were alone in their attempt to start a baby program. Most had never heard of any other company that allowed babies to come in. When MAYA Design was considering whether to allow an employee (who was pregnant at the time) to bring her baby to the office, the HR manager, Terry Pronko, searched to find a policy on parents bringing babies to work. After some research, Terry came back with the comment, "There isn't a policy on this, anywhere—no one is doing this." So MAYA decided to create their own policy. They were so pleased with the results that they decided to continue the program with other babies.

As COO Wendy Zanotelli explains, the first time a baby program was proposed at UNCLE Credit Union at the

executive level, she said no. She said that she didn't want
babies on the teller line because she thought it would
detract from the service level they could provide. But, she
said, the second time the topic came up, proponents of the
idea convinced her, and now she is "one of the biggest
supporters of it." She said:

> Other companies have had hesitation [in
> deciding to start a program]. I'm the best
> one to talk to; my advice is to try it out. If it
> doesn't work, you can always take it away.
> But the benefits of the program far outweigh
> the negatives.

Cathy Weatherford said that, when she proposed
allowing babies to come to work at the National
Association of Insurance Commissioners (NAIC):

> Some of my direct reports thought I was off
> my rocker when I said I wanted to do this.
> But I asked them to be helpful and to give it
> a try—and if it didn't work, we'd let it go.
> Some of the biggest naysayers became some
> of the biggest champions when they found
> that, from just giving a little bit, we were
> retaining important staff members who were
> big contributors [to the business]. It has
> been a very, very positive program for our
> workplace.

Sally Rynne, the founder of Health Newsletters Direct,
said that her company had about twelve employees when
they first decided to allow a baby to come to work. A
company-wide meeting was held to discuss this new policy.
One of the newer employees, a younger man who worked

for the new mom, was clearly upset. He said to Sally, who was leading the meeting, "What am I supposed to think? There's my boss with a baby in her arms." He seemed to expect Sally to be equally appalled and say something like, "You're right—oh my, what were we thinking?" Instead, she looked at him and calmly replied, "And soooo, what?" The employee couldn't respond—he couldn't actually think of a logical reason why the happy baby shouldn't be there except that it was something he had never seen before.

Similar situations occurred in nearly every one of the baby-friendly companies when the idea of allowing babies was first proposed. Since people had never before heard of parents bringing babies to work, and because they assumed that babies by nature cry frequently and for long periods of time, most people assumed that a parent trying to work with a baby was destined to fail.

Our culture has excluded babies and children from the work environment for so long that we've forgotten that, for most of the human race's existence and even in some societies today, babies and children are just part of a typical day—and that both children and adults can thrive with this integration.

## Converted

Once the decision had been made to allow babies at the Kansas Insurance Department, Brian Moline decided to make the most of the situation. He realized that the legal department was the best place to test the program, since two attorneys were pregnant at the time. When, a few months later, the first baby came to work, Brian quickly became the program's biggest supporter. He discovered that he was "the biggest sap in the world" when it came to these work babies. The first baby spent a lot of time in her walker and regularly would travel from her mother's cubicle to Brian's office to visit him.

Brian's secretary's work area had a low wall over which she could see into his office. One day, she heard Brian saying things like, "Go away. I'm not doing it. You may as well just go away." But there didn't appear to be anyone in his office. For a few minutes, she thought he had gone crazy and was talking to himself. Then she realized that the baby was in Brian's office doorway, in her walker, with her arms outstretched for Brian to hold her as he regularly did throughout the day.

By the time Brian moved to another Kansas agency, he was such a big supporter of babies in the workplace that he spearheaded the implementation of a babies-at-work program at the new agency. (More than 20 state agencies in Kansas now have active babies-at-work programs.)

## Babies At Work Are Highly Content

It turns out that the majority of babies in the more than 100 baby-friendly companies cry very infrequently and are actually extremely content. Nathan Schmidt, of Schools Financial, said that, when the baby policy was first implemented:

> The managers were really concerned, especially in branch locations—about the money, the members, the teller lines. They said it wouldn't work. But it does work.

Debbie Butler, of Valley Credit Union, said, "In the past, people thought there were certain departments in which having a baby wouldn't work at all." But she said that, over the years, people in many of those "inappropriate" positions successfully brought in their babies, and now she thinks that "most positions are feasible for having a baby." As an example, she mentioned that people used to think that it would be impossible to have a baby in the IT (computer) department. Then one of the programmers proved that assumption wrong by bringing his daughter to work with him three days a week. He simply wore the baby in a front carrier or backpack while he worked at the computer.

Deborah Driskill, of CDG & Associates, noted that "the babies were not very fussy, because they were with their mothers." Carolyn Gable of New Age Transportation and Willie Jones of Magical Journey Bookstore both commented that not one of the babies who came to work at their companies was colicky. Willie attributed this to the fact that, "the only time the babies were not being held was when they were asleep." Carolyn adds, "They have their mom and everyone else. They feel that they are loved."

Too often we mistakenly assume that babies' physical helplessness means that they do not have emotional and intellectual needs. In reality, babies are tremendously intelligent and socially aware even at birth, and they crave social interaction and emotional nurturing just like older children and adults. When we understand and fulfill those needs (as well as their physical needs), healthy babies have little reason to cry—they have everything they require to be happy.

| 9 | Top Ten Tips for A Successful Baby Program |
|---|---|
| | Give Parent a Transition Period |

# 3

# WHY IT WORKS

## Responsive Care Creates Happy Babies

One key reason that babies at work are so content is that, in well-structured programs, parents quickly respond to their babies' cries in order to keep the babies content and to avoid disturbing coworkers, as well as to allow the parents to efficiently get work done. Mary Admasian explained that crying really wasn't a problem for most of the babies that have come to work at Zutano, a designer and manufacturer of children's clothing and toys. She said, "the babies do cry, but when they are close to mom and mom pays attention, it's usually not an issue. It depends on the quality of the parent as well." These babies learned that they could trust their parents and that they did not have to cry very long to get their needs met.

Babies usually start out whimpering or making quiet sounds of unhappiness when they need help. If a caretaker responds quickly to these requests and solves the baby's problem, in most cases the baby never has a reason to resort to full-blown screaming. If the babies' cries are ignored, however (since crying is the only method babies have of communicating their distress), they will steadily cry louder and more insistently in a desperate attempt to get the help they need. Eventually the baby's need is met and the baby returns to equilibrium and contentment. But the next time the baby is uncomfortable or scared, he has learned that he won't be helped until he cries loudly and for a long time. Since he can't return to contentment until his need is met, he does what he thinks will get the need met more quickly. So, the longer a caregiver waits to meet a baby's needs, the more frequently and the longer the baby will scream in the future. At the same time, the baby who has to repeatedly scream for long periods to get his needs met is steadily learning that he can't trust people to take care of him, which affects his view of his own value as a person and his trust in his caregivers.

Dr. Meredith Small, a professor of anthropology at Cornell University, wrote a carefully documented, enlightening book called *Our Babies, Ourselves: How Biology and Culture Shape the Way We Parent*, which discusses cross-cultural parenting styles and the data on the impact of various practices on the babies themselves, and explains a great deal about why babies in our society cry so much more than babies in cultures with more "attachment-based" parenting styles. The book explains why babies are born so helpless and what babies expect from their parents from an anthropological perspective. Humans are primates. Other primates—gorillas, for example—are able to cling to their mothers' bodies immediately after birth and hang on while the mothers are traveling. Human infants are born unable to even control their own hand movements—they are completely vulnerable and dependent on other people to meet every need.

The reasons for this, as Dr. Small explains, are the abnormally large brains humans have relative to our body size and the pelvic bone structure that allows humans to walk on only two limbs instead of using four legs like most other primates. Dr. Small goes into considerable detail on the mechanics behind this but, basically, human babies are born neurologically premature. If a human baby stayed in his mother's body until the point of being more self-sufficient at birth like other primates, his head would be too big for his mother to safely give birth. Human babies are essentially born too soon due to the fact that we walk on two legs. This idea is also the basis of many of the concepts in Dr. Harvey Karp's book *The Happiest Baby on the Block: The New Way to Calm Crying and Help Your Newborn Baby Sleep Longer*, which details highly-effective methods used in indigenous cultures for calming young babies through mimicking the environment of the womb.

A baby is born expecting her every need to be met immediately. For the previous nine months she was in a calm, warm, safe environment in which every physical need was continuously met through her umbilical cord. From a biological perspective, babies wouldn't even be outside their mothers at nine months if humans had never started walking upright. Breastfeeding and close physical contact help considerably to continue the baby's normal development, as do parents who respond quickly when the baby asks for help.

The human impulse to respond immediately to a baby's cries is evident from a biological perspective. Mothers (and fathers, but it's often more intense for mothers) are biologically driven to soothe their babies and meet their needs. Have you ever seen the mother of an infant when her baby is screaming but the mother is unable to help the baby—for example, if the baby is crying in the back seat while the mother is driving? For many mothers, being unable to soothe their babies is excruciating—and often results in the mothers breaking into tears as well. Most mothers react extremely strongly to their babies' cries—not because the sound is painful in itself, but because every part of a mother's being is telling her to help her baby *now*.

While it might seem strange for us to have such a visceral response to a baby's cry, from an evolutionary perspective, it makes perfect sense. Before cities really got off the ground, so to speak, humans lived off the land in social groups, helping each other to find food, helping to defend the group from animal predators, and assisting each other in day-to-day survival tasks. Simply finding enough food, water, and shelter to survive took up most of their time. In order for babies to stay fed and have their needs met, they had to be able to communicate those needs and a parent had to be motivated enough to pause in their survival tasks to take care of the baby. In addition, in that kind of environment it was critical that a baby *not* cry loudly or for long periods of time because the sound would have attracted predators to the group. A baby's cry thus evolved along with a mother's hormones such that mothers feel a tremendous compulsion to meet their babies' needs quickly to stop the crying. The psychological bond between babies and parents that is created through months of responsive communication and close contact is designed to encourage parents to care for their young, and the trust and attachment that the baby develops with her parents provides the model for healthy relationships with other people as she grows into adulthood. Regine Schön of the University of Helsinki recently published an incredibly thorough and interesting analysis of the extensive data documenting these principles and others described in this book (available online at www.epjournal.net/filestore/ep05102183.pdf).

However, in recent decades our society has come to expect newborn babies to be self-reliant almost as soon as they are born. The idea still permeates our culture that responding immediately when a baby cries will "spoil" the child, that they will never learn delayed gratification, and that they will never learn to be independent. As a society that prides itself on self-reliance, we want our children to grow up to be self-sufficient. So we do things as we raise our children that we think will encourage this outcome. We still place babies into cribs away from their mothers immediately after birth, and doctors routinely encourage parents to make their babies sleep alone from day one. But if we look at the history of humanity and baby biology, it turns out that these expectations are completely unrealistic for human babies—and that this kind of care is a significant reason that most babies in our society cry so much.

Scientific and psychological studies are making it clear that close physical contact and responsive care are actually critical for normal psychological and physical development. In the short term, regularly ignoring a baby's cries for help leads to more crying, and long term it leads to difficulty handling stress and difficulty forming healthy relationships as an adult, as well as other psychological (and sometimes physical) problems. The book *The Science of Parenting* by Professor Margot Sunderland explains the data on the importance of touch and responsive care, as well as the risks of brain damage if a child is intentionally left to cry (particularly if they are left *alone* to cry) for long periods.

If most babies in the office screamed for hours on end, babies-at-work programs would last for about one day. This is where the structure of baby programs becomes important. When parents know that their babies' participation in the program is contingent on coworkers not being disturbed, parents respond immediately to the slightest sound of distress—thus tapping in to a key component of happy, healthy babies that our society lost sight of many years ago.

## Babies Love Physical Contact

Nearly-constant physical contact is another reason that babies in the workplace cry far less than the stereotypical baby in our society. Not only do babies enjoy lots of physical contact with other people; they need it for normal development. In some cultures, babies are almost constantly held in a sling on their mothers' (or other community members') bodies while the mothers work, so the babies automatically receive the extensive physical contact that we now know is crucial for proper physical and psychological development. Parents in these countries are baffled, for example, as to why strollers are so prevalent in our society; they can't understand why we would want to keep our babies so far away from us. Their views on baby-rearing have not been clouded by self-appointed "experts" who for decades have told us to ignore our instincts about keeping our babies close (by telling us that they would become spoiled or "too attached"). Our society is only recently starting to become aware of the data that our instincts reflect exactly what babies need, and that extensive physical contact and responsive care of babies actually lead to healthier, happier, and *more* independent and self-sufficient children and adults.

Most babies who come to the workplace often receive extensive physical contact just like the babies in indigenous cultures. These workplace babies are generally right next to their mother or father all day long or being held by a coworker. In many cases, the parents hold the babies in carriers or on their laps while they work, so the babies feel secure and happy. Sandy Jaffe, owner of The Booksource, noted that, "These babies were held more than normal— you'd walk in and see the receptionist just holding her baby and doing her job."

Wendy Zanotelli said that babies can come to work at UNCLE Credit Union "as soon as the doctor releases mom or dad and baby to come. One baby started at six weeks old. He spent a lot of time in a front pack. It went great." If these babies made any sounds of discomfort, the parents (or coworkers) were right there to immediately meet the babies' needs.

Studies have clearly shown that holding babies more leads to them crying less. One key study (available online at www.portareipiccoli.it/trial_hunziker.htm) explained:

> We conclude that supplemental carrying modifies "normal" crying by reducing the duration and altering the typical pattern of crying and fussing in the first 3 months of life. The relative lack of carrying in our society may predispose to crying and colic in normal infants.

This makes perfect sense since, as mentioned, colic doesn't even exist in cultures in which babies are carried pretty much constantly during the day, their needs are met within seconds, they are breastfed frequently, and they sleep next to their mother at night (co-sleeping with infants is actually the norm in most of the world). To people in these cultures, the "normal" prolonged crying of many of our babies is inconceivable.

Not only is it physically and emotionally healthy for babies to be frequently held and touched, but babies' strong desire to be carried by another person makes sense in another way as well. Scientific studies of babies make clear that babies are far more intelligent and aware of their world than previously believed—they want to be involved in the world so that they can learn as much as possible. The book *The Scientist in the Crib: What Early Learning Tells Us About the Mind*, by Dr. Alison Gopnik, Dr. Andrew N. Meltzoff, and Dr. Patricia K. Kuhl, goes into fascinating detail on babies' incredible abilities to learn language and other social cues. For example, only a few minutes after birth, a baby can mimic another person sticking out his tongue. As the book explains, this is actually incredible when you consider that the baby has never before seen a human being. In order to imitate, she has to have the ability to differentiate a human face from the rest of her surroundings *and* she has to understand on some level that *she looks like that too.* Babies appear to be born with innate knowledge of their humanness. Babies are also aware of and begin learning language even before they are born. They pay incredibly close attention to what goes on around them—especially other people's words and actions—much more than many people realize.

Holding babies or wearing them in a sling or wrap-style baby carrier is ideal for their physical development and gives them the perfect vantage point for observing the world. They are close to eye level with other people and can see everything that is going on around them. They are able to see other people's faces and watch and learn from the interactions between people. People interact with them more frequently because the babies are in easy view. Babies want interaction with other humans so that they can learn how to interact. We know that children and adults enjoy communicating and interacting with each other—why would we think that babies would be any different?

My younger daughter illustrated to me how deeply babies crave new information—sometimes even more than basic survival needs. When she was three weeks old, I once had to drive for eight hours with her and her older sister. I stopped periodically to nurse the baby but, aside from those brief stops, I drove pretty much nonstop. The baby was too young to hold or really notice small objects and so the only things she had to look at when I was driving were her sister and the view from her rear-facing car seat. Each time I tried to breastfeed her, she would only nurse for a few moments and then would lift her head up to look around the front of the car and the scenery outside. She spent long periods of time observing everything around her and it was extremely difficult for me to convince her that there was food available. All she wanted to do was observe her world. She probably nursed for a total of 20 minutes during the eight-hour trip—and then nursed for a very long time when we finally reached our destination. Even though she must have been ravenous during the trip, getting her stimulation needs met was more important to her.

When many babies in our society leave the house, they are carried in infant car seats or put on their backs in a stroller. For many, all they can see is the sky (if they're lucky), the ceiling, or other people's legs. It's perfectly logical that most of these stroller and car seat babies always seem to be crying; they're bored and are begging for something to look at so that they can learn. Babies who are held more cry far less, not only because they feel safe and secure but because this gives them more opportunities for learning about and interacting with their world. This is another reason that babies at work are so "unusually" happy—in many cases, they become very engaged in watching their parents' (and other people's) activities, and their craving to learn is satisfied.

## Babies Love Social Interaction

As mentioned, the workplace is often a very socially interesting and stimulating place for a baby. Babies are born able to recognize human faces and they show far more interest in looking at faces than at anything else. Babies love to be around lots of different people, to watch people interacting with each other, and to learn as much as possible about their world. The best way for a baby to do this is to be immersed in human activity—to be around people and to be able to watch their day-to-day activities (as well as to have their physical needs met quickly so that they can focus their energy on learning).

*The Scientist in the Crib* theorizes that one reason that human children have such a long period of dependence (more than any other species) is to give them a protected period in which to learn the nuances and details of their particular culture and environment. As the authors of the book explain, this is a key reason that humans are so adaptable (we can thrive under far more diverse conditions than virtually any other species) and why we have been able to achieve the technological advances and intricate societies of modern times.

As any new parent knows, when babies are awake they require nearly-constant stimulation to be content. This is extremely difficult for one person to provide; many adults have trouble thinking of new and interesting things to do with a baby for eight to ten hours a day. The pattern seen in more community-based cultures (and the success of babies-at-work programs) strongly suggests that babies are not meant to interact with only one person for the majority of each day.  Since the beginning of the human species, people lived in groups for protection, companionship, and to divide the burdens of survival tasks.  Babies are meant to take advantage of and to learn from this social interaction.  From a biological and societal perspective, they may not be at their best being isolated for long periods of time with only one person, and particularly not spending many hours in a stroller or a crib at daycare with little to look at but the ceiling or toys for much of their day.  Kandace Bozarth of Schools Financial Credit Union explained that:

> [My daughter] got bored with toys in minutes, but if I had her sitting with me in the teller booth, she would be entertained for hours on my lap just hanging out with everyone.  She would get tired, take a nap, wake up, eat, and then watch people some more.

As Kandace discovered firsthand, babies are far more interested in watching and learning from other people than they are in playing with manufactured toys.  Credit union tellers and retail employees who brought their babies to work discovered that their babies stayed content for hours just sitting on their parents' laps, watching the parents work, and interacting with customers and coworkers.  The same phenomenon was seen in all of the businesses with active babies-at-work policies.  If a baby did cry to have a need met and the parent was unable to immediately stop working to take care of the situation, one or more coworkers would eagerly come to the rescue and pick up the baby or otherwise meet the baby's needs.  These babies had lots of friendly people who talked to and frequently interacted with them and who came to feel invested in the welfare and happiness of these children in their vicinity.

Ted Gerber at Foris Winery commented about the children who came to work, "There's enough activity that they can be entertained just by watching people work." Wendy Zanotelli of UNCLE Credit Union explained:

> One baby was pretty fussy for the first week, and we thought we would have a problem. But he became socialized, and there were lots of people around and cooing at him. For the next week and from then on, he was absolutely fine. I think [being in the workplace] helps babies become better adjusted. It was a huge thing I noticed— being around lots of people makes babies happy.

Just as they cry to indicate hunger or the need for a diaper change, many babies kept inside with only one adult, or left in cribs at daycare facilities, cry out of boredom. They are asking, in the only way they can, for more stimulation to meet the needs of their rapidly growing minds. Babies who are carried constantly in indigenous cultures are at the eye level of the people around them and easily see and learn about their environment. Since they spend their days with their parents and other members of the society as chores are done and people interact with each other, they have plenty of opportunities to learn about human behavior and cultural norms, just as they are meant to do.

Babies start being able to consistently hold onto and interact with objects on their own at around six months of age. Prior to that time, their primary method of learning is through observation of other children, adults, and the world around them. It makes sense, given the huge growth that their brains go through during this time, that they would crave frequent and varied types of stimulation. Babies go from being completely dependent and helpless at birth to being able to pick up and manipulate objects, sit up on their own, and sometimes even learn the extremely complicated skill of crawling—all in only six months. By the time they are a year old, many can walk (also a very difficult and impressive feat) and some even know how to say various words. The amount of learning babies do is absolutely incredible—and they need lots of time and opportunities to make the most of their potential.

Numerous times when she was under six months old, my younger daughter would start to be fussy if we stayed in the house all day—but literally the second I took her outside she would stop crying and could spend hours in my arms just observing the larger world. She had already seen what the inside of the house looked like and, since she wasn't old enough to interact on her own with toys or other items, the only way she could learn more (aside from directly interacting with another person) was to be physically moved to a new place with new things—and, ideally, new people—to look at. Many new parents have also noticed that their baby can be crying or generally unhappy for hours if she's at home with only one adult and familiar surroundings. But if they take her outside, or shopping, or to some other environment with lots of different people and things to look at, suddenly the baby is perfectly content. Some parents are unaware of this dynamic and they stay at home *because* their baby is crying and they don't want the baby to disturb other people by going out in public.

Unfortunately, this often means that the baby remains bored and continues to cry.

As I was researching the issues related to babies in the workplace and coming to understand just how much babies love being part of human interactions, I tested this "boredom" theory. Several times when I was out in public and saw a baby crying in a stroller or car seat (I never actually saw one crying who was being held in a carrier or in someone's arms), I would go close to the baby (with the parent's permission) and start talking to the child. *Every time*, the baby would immediately stop crying and would smile and make facial expressions in an attempt to communicate. On one occasion. I was with a friend who was caring for a very fussy four-month-old baby. He was starting to work himself into a fairly distressed state and my friend said, "Once he gets like this, nothing works to make him happy." I knelt down next to where the baby was sitting in a bouncy seat and started talking to him in a happy, excited voice. He immediately and completely stopped crying, smiled, and started moving his arms and making facial expressions in clear response to my words. As long as I interacted with him. he was completely content. I suggested to my friend that the baby appeared to have extremely high needs for stimulation—and she commented that he did seem to remain happy as long as he had lots of activities to observe.

Our society seems to feel that, because babies can't clearly express their desires for human interaction and contact, they don't need these things. The prevalence in our society of keeping babies in covered strollers when they are awake is a good indicator of this belief. There seems to be an assumption in our culture that, until babies are able to crawl or walk, they are unthinking beings who aren't interested in anything except eating and sleeping. But the truth is, babies have tremendous potential and desire to learn about their world from the moment they are born—and the more opportunities we give them to make use of that potential, the happier (and more intelligent) they will be. Simply carrying a baby in a carrier or in your arms (whenever possible) is a powerful method of raising a happy, healthy, intelligent baby who will feel engaged and connected to the world.

Babies in indigenous cultures are generally held all day. A mother with her baby may do household chores, talk with others in the community, do farming tasks, or spend a lot of time outside where there are likely to be other children and possibly animals to look at. These mothers don't have much leisure time in which they can focus solely on their babies. The babies don't have access to the huge array of toys that our babies do. Yet these babies are content and never cry for any substantial length of time—largely because they feel like active participants in society. The same social dynamic occurs in babies-at-work programs.

## Community Parenting

Happy babies invariably create a community dynamic in companies with structured baby programs. Coworkers and often even executives in these companies automatically pitch in to support parents and babies by playing with a baby for a few minutes at a time or taking a baby for a walk when the parent needs to devote all of her attention to a project. Babies at work have lots of people who care about them and who can distribute the tasks of playing with, talking to, and holding them.

In addition, bringing their babies to work often gives new parents a built-in support network in their coworkers, which often helps them to deal more effectively with the stressful moments and work involved in new parenthood. Parents bringing their babies to work often appreciate the opportunity to have adult conversations and social interaction instead of feeling isolated at home with their babies. Many coworkers enjoy the opportunity to see and play with happy babies as a stress reliever during their work day, and they become emotionally invested in helping to nurture these little people.

This "community parenting" phenomenon contradicts many people's prior expectations about babies at work. People often object to babies in the workplace in theory, often based on a general sentiment that they "don't want to deal with other people's children." It actually makes a lot of sense that our society has so much resistance to the idea of working with kids close by. We live in a culture in which many adults without children have little or no experience or one-on-one interaction with babies. For many, their impression of babies is often focused on their memories of screaming babies on airplanes or in restaurants. It's no surprise that they worry about a similar situation being replicated in the workplace.

In structured work programs, though, the reality is far different from what many people imagine. First of all, babies at work are usually highly content, and policy rules ensure that, in the rare situation that a baby can't be soothed in a few seconds, the parent temporarily removes the baby from the vicinity of coworkers until the baby is again quiet and happy. The result is that coworkers' experiences with these babies are usually highly positive.

In indigenous cultures (and for most of human history), as mentioned, an integrated community structure develops in which men and women all contribute their skills to sustain and build their society and to raise children at the same time. Because children stay with their parents as they perform societal tasks, they have the opportunity to develop individual relationships with other adults (and children) in the community, and those adults become emotionally attached to the children and feel a sense of personal responsibility for their happiness and well-being.

In workplace baby programs, the same dynamic occurs. Work colleagues become the "tribe" and a sense of mutual investment develops for most people. Humans actually have an instinctive nurturing response to children—particularly babies. A recent study at Oxford University found that simply seeing a baby's face triggers a "sense of reward and good feeling" in just one-seventh of a second. In other words, part of our brain is actually hard-wired to make us feel happy and calm when we look at a baby.

Instead of feeling disconnected from "other people's children," coworkers in companies with structured baby programs end up developing personal relationships with the babies—who, after all, are individuals who crave social connections as much as any adult. Far from resenting the babies' presence, in practice most coworkers become excited about the opportunity to briefly interact with and hold these tiny, innocent beings who, ultimately, ask for nothing more than love.

## Breastfeeding Means Happier
## and Healthier Babies

Bringing a baby to work makes it much easier for a
mother to breastfeed and to continue breastfeeding longer
than she otherwise might have—which means happier
babies. As most breastfeeding mothers can attest, nursing
is usually a first resort for comforting a distraught baby—as
it is biologically intended to be. Although distressed babies
can generally (eventually) be comforted by rocking or
singing or distracting them in other ways, nursing is an
extremely effective tool.

Mary Admasian of Zutano explained that most of the
mothers who have brought their babies to work breastfed
them and that "babies who breastfeed don't cry as much
(unless they are teething)." Alicia Lionberger at Foris
Winery nursed her baby at work. As she said, "It definitely
made it easier. While I was on the phone with customers,
nursing kept him happy." Dana Croy, who brought her
baby to work at Magical Journey, corroborated this,
commenting that:

> Nursing is really a key to taking a baby to
> work. It's an instant baby soother for most
> babies. It also meant I didn't have to take
> extra time to make a bottle and didn't have
> to tote a lot of extra things with me like
> formula.

Babies don't just breastfeed for food; breastfeeding is a
natural method of comforting a baby and it also has many
other benefits. Since babies are "born too soon" from a
biological standpoint, breastfeeding helps tremendously to
continue a baby's normal development. The composition of

human milk actually changes from day to day to accommodate the specific needs of the growing child's system, so breastfeeding means fewer digestive problems for a baby. Contrary to the "scheduled" feeding model that was prevalent a few decades ago (which can cause problems with milk production and often leads to a much fussier baby), babies left to their own devices usually nurse briefly at frequent intervals.

When a baby breastfeeds, germs that are in the baby's system are passed to the mother, whose body makes antibodies for those germs and then passes the antibodies back to the baby as he nurses. Breastfeeding is a biological mechanism for protecting children from illness and infection and building a strong lifelong immune system—which is a key reason that breastfed babies get sick far less often and less severely than babies who are not nursed. In fact, studies have shown that for every 1,000 babies who are not breastfed, there are 2,000 additional doctor visits, 600 more prescriptions, and 200 more hospitalization days.

Babies who are *not* breastfed are more likely to suffer from ear and respiratory infections, have a higher risk of succumbing to Sudden Infant Death Syndrome and developing certain kinds of cancer and diabetes, as well as being more likely to develop allergies and asthma. Several studies have indicated that breastfed babies have higher IQs (which makes sense given that human milk is important for optimal brain development). Scientists have even discovered that human milk can directly kill cancer cells. Frequent breastfeeding helps to maintain the proper fat content in human milk to keep a baby satiated, as well as helping to maintain the mother's milk supply (since the more frequently a baby nurses, the more milk the mother's body produces).

The extensive benefits from frequent breastfeeding may explain (from an anthropological viewpoint) why babies have such a strong desire to suck. This also helps to explain why pacifiers are relied on so heavily in our culture—a pacifier is, in effect, a substitute for the very-frequent breastfeeding that is common in indigenous cultures. Babies in the workplace who are able to nurse frequently (particularly if they exclusively have human milk for the first six months of life, as recommended by a number of major child development organizations) are less likely to get sick or to have digestive pain, are more easily comforted, and are more likely to feel satisfied and content.

Although a number of formula-fed babies have been successfully brought to work in these companies, the higher rates of breastfeeding made possible by these programs contribute greatly to the happiness of many babies at work.

## Babies Sleep Frequently and Parents Make It Work

Parents who participate in these baby programs become extremely grateful to their companies for giving them the chance to have those extra few months with their babies before shifting to another arrangement. As a result, these parents feel tremendous loyalty toward their companies and they work hard to show their gratitude. This is a major reason that structured baby programs work so well. As Carolyn Gable of New Age puts it, "The parents go out of their way to make it work." Carolyn said that the parents were ultra-conscious of making sure that the babies didn't disrupt the work environment. She said that, when babies started getting too active or too fussy, "the parents are the ones that say, 'I need to get a babysitter.' They know when it's not working."

Parents in these programs are generally anxious to avoid letting their baby's presence disturb coworkers, as well as careful to get their work done effectively and efficiently. They put forth extra effort because they want to ensure that they will be able to continue bringing their baby to work, and because they want to give back to the organization that gave them such a priceless opportunity.

Parents' efforts to balance baby care and work are made easier by the fact that babies sleep much of the time during the first few months of life (particularly if they are close to another person and feel safe and secure as a result). Parents in the workplace make the most of their babies' naps to get work done as efficiently as possible. Many parents who bring their babies to work keep them in baby carriers or on their laps for much of each day. When the babies are awake, their parents and other people are readily available to meet their needs.

## Many of Today's Jobs Allow Task Flexibility

The Industrial Revolution marked the beginning of the only period in human history in which babies have been separated from their mothers on a routine basis while the mothers were working. This was primarily due to the fact that the women in the workforce at the time were usually in factories. A factory environment was unsafe for children and, from a practical standpoint, it would have been difficult to effectively care for a baby while working on an assembly line.

But our current technology-based economy is a different world from the perspective of having children around. Now, many office (and some retail) jobs are structured in such a way that parents can effectively do their work and care for a baby at the same time. In this Information Age, creativity and resourcefulness are highly-prized traits in employees, and many employees have tremendous flexibility in the specific way in which they do their jobs. These modern conditions make working while caring for a baby highly feasible in many cases, and the assistance of willing coworkers in an office environment can help parents be even more effective at doing their jobs than they might be by telecommuting from home while taking care of children all by themselves.

## Formal Structure and Limited Duration

A big key to the success of these baby programs is having clear guidelines and expectations (and preferably a detailed, formal policy, particularly in larger organizations). The concept of babies in the workplace has been discussed in a number of internet forums in recent years. People's comments seem to fall into three groups. The first group consists of people who are opposed to the idea because they've never seen it in practice and just assume (based on their stereotyped beliefs about babies) that it can't possibly work. The second group includes people who are opposed to the idea because they had isolated negative experiences with their own or other people's babies being brought to the office on an informal, occasional basis (with no formal procedures or expectations in place to prevent problems). The third group encompasses people who successfully took their own babies to work and, notably, people who work for a company with a formal, structured program. In this third group, there is virtually unanimous support for having babies in the workplace.

Partially because many in our society still believe that babies inherently cry for hours on end, the idea of babies in the workplace can be daunting. But the dynamics of structured baby programs are highly conducive to keeping babies happy and calm, and the nature of many of our current jobs is conducive to parenting while working— especially when participating parents understand baby psychology and biology.

Although a few companies allow babies to come to work until a year of age (or older, in some cases), the majority of companies with baby programs limit a baby's stay to approximately six to eight months of age or crawling, whichever comes first. Monitoring a crawling child while trying to work is far more difficult than caring for a stationary baby, and a toddler wandering around an office can create higher risks from a business standpoint. Having this "mobility" limitation as part of their official baby policy allows companies to compromise between helping their employees to balance family obligations and ensuring that work still gets done and safety and liability risks are minimized.

To a large degree, a successful baby program is like any other business policy. For example, few companies could function effectively with a free-for-all vacation policy, in which employees could choose not to work at all for a random week with no prior notice to the company. These baby programs work because companies put effort into creating a sustainable program that works beautifully most of the time and they have provisions in place to effectively handle the rare complication that might arise.

| 8 | Top Ten Tips for A Successful Baby Program |
|---|---|
| | Be Ready to Resolve Issues |

# 4

# BENEFITS FOR FAMILIES

Years ago, I saw a picture of an African
woman. She was walking on a pile of trees
that had fallen. She had her baby in a sling
on her back as she balanced more logs on her
head. When I saw that, I thought, "If she can
do that, I can do anything."
                    Peggy O'Mara
                    Editor of *Mothering Magazine*

## Lower Stress For Parents

By having their babies with them at work, parents do not
endure the stress of separation from their young infants or
the constant worrying about whether they are safe and
happy at daycare. Lower stress means better health for
parents.

Jeff Miller said that he was grateful to The Booksource
because:

> [They gave me] the opportunity to [bring my
> baby to work] instead of sticking a child into
> daycare at that age. It's scary to me that he

would have been in that environment
without me there at all at such a young age.

Jackie Hockaday of Austin, Texas, brought her baby to work. She said that:

I can't say enough from a mother's point of
view to be able to do this. It means the
world to me—and to my husband. He is
pleased that our baby gets to be with me.

Kim Martin, also of Austin, explained that, "one of the things mothers worry about most when they are pregnant is what they will do when they have to go back to work." She said that, "knowing [my babies] could come with me took stress off—there wasn't a fear of the unknown." She added that she was "still trying to learn how to be a mom anyway, so it was nice not to have to break from them so soon." When a baby is in daycare for forty or fifty hours a week, many of the baby milestones can happen when a parent isn't there to witness them. Jackie Hockaday explained that:

[I] got to see my son roll over for the first
time here [at work]. I didn't with my first
child; it was a huge deal for me. It was one
of those things I caught out of the corner of
my eye while answering an email.

Mary Admasian mentioned that Zutano believes that it is very important for parents to be able to be with their child during that first year, since babies grow so fast (babies at Zutano can come to work until they are one year old). As Mary noted, "babies change hourly." Being part of these magical moments can mean the world to parents.

36

Baby programs also help women to more easily balance their often-competing roles. The feminist movement was a revolution in women's beliefs and opportunities in our society; it helped large numbers of women feel empowered to enter the workforce and pursue active professional careers. But many women feel as though there is something wrong with them whether they choose to stay home with their children or they choose to postpone having children (or don't have them at all) and instead focus on directly contributing in the economic world. Also, many mothers have no financial alternative but to work outside the home and they often feel highly conflicted about being away from their babies so much. Taking babies to work bridges these divisions. Women who can participate in a baby program no longer need to worry or feel guilty if they miss the intellectual stimulation of their jobs several weeks after their baby is born; they can just return to work and bring their baby with them.

## Happier Marriages

Some couples work opposing schedules to minimize the amount of time their baby is in daycare. This can put stress on marriages since these couples are rarely able to spend much awake time together during the work week. If one parent (or both) can take the baby to work, parents can work the same schedule and thus have more time together as a family.

Another way that baby programs help to strengthen marriages is by helping parents to minimize daycare expenses because their baby can come to work. Money is a major source of conflict for many couples, and infant daycare is often extremely expensive. In addition, having to leave her new baby to go to work can create tremendous stress and anxiety for a mother, which can spill over into her relationship with her partner.

A baby program also enables women to more easily transition back to their jobs and lowers the likelihood that they will feel compelled to quit their jobs rather than put their newborn babies in daycare. In our current economic climate, having only one income can put a tremendous financial strain on a family. If a mother takes her baby to work, she can continue to contribute to her family's financial stability while still being able to bond with and nurture her child.

## Easier Breastfeeding Equals Healthier Babies and Mothers

Many new mothers have little or no assistance in learning how to breastfeed their babies, and without continued social support and encouragement from lactation support professionals or from other mothers, many quit nursing in the first several weeks of their baby's life or soon after returning to work.

For many women, returning to work—or even the prospect of returning to work—discourages breastfeeding. Even part-time work (without taking the baby along or having on-site daycare) has been shown to decrease the length of time a mother nurses. Continuing to nurse after they return to work without their baby generally requires pumping at least two or three times throughout the day, often more. Pumps are less effective than a nursing baby at extracting milk, so, especially in those early months, some mothers are unable to get enough milk through pumping to keep up their milk supply and to fully meet their babies' needs while at daycare. Many of these mothers either wean their babies early or end up needing to supplement with formula, which can make for fussier and sicker babies because formula is harder to digest and has none of the immune system benefits of human milk. Being able to bring a baby to work makes it far easier for a mother to successfully breastfeed and she is thus more likely to initiate breastfeeding and continue nursing for longer.

Sally Rynne commented that, at Health Newsletters Direct, there was "a lot of breastfeeding going on." Sally said that part of the rationale of allowing babies in the first place was "to encourage and make it easy for moms to breastfeed." She said that bringing a baby to work gave moms an opportunity to get support, especially about nursing issues. She explained that it can be "tough for new moms to feel confident enough—they wonder whether they should supplement, whether they should nurse every hour and a half, things like that." She said that there was discussion of parenting issues among coworkers "that was just natural because the baby was there." Sally added that "there were women who wanted to nurse in spite of the fact that it wasn't going well, and they got support [from their coworkers]" in pursuing that goal. Having coworkers readily available to answer questions about nursing difficulties or to suggest ideas and resources can also be a tremendous benefit for mothers in the workplace.

Sonya Allen of the Office of the State Banking Commissioner in Kansas greatly appreciated the ease of nursing her baby at work. She said that:

> If you can have the convenience of having
> [the baby] right there, it would encourage
> you to nurse them. Even if you pump, it's

not as efficient as a baby, and it's time
consuming.

Kerry Olson said that the baby program at the North
Dakota Department of Health first started in the Maternal
and Child Health Division. He explained that the Division
looked at it as a good way to enable mothers to continue to
breastfeed. He said that a lot of mothers in the program
nursed, and he thinks "that has a lot to do with bringing in a
child. Most mothers who breastfeed appreciate being able
to continue when they come back to work."

Even if a mother only brings her baby to work on a part-
time basis, breastfeeding on those days will help her to
maintain her milk supply and will make it easier for her to
pump enough milk for when her baby is with his father or
another caregiver. Since human milk can be safely frozen
for about six months, a baby program also makes it easier
for a working mother to pump as well as nurse (if she
chooses) and freeze the milk for use when her baby moves
to a different care arrangement.

Given the extensive short-term and long-term benefits
for babies and mothers from breastfeeding for at least six
months (and potentially much longer, as is the biological
norm for our species) instead of receiving only man-made
baby formula, this aspect of baby programs can be a
tremendous benefit for families.

## Easier Bonding

Being able to take their babies to work means that
parents can spend more time with their children and thus
form a stronger bond. Jackie Hockaday said that it was
really important to her that she was able to bring her second

son to work. She said that she felt as though she was not able to really bond with her first son since she had to return to work so soon and that, even though her second baby could only come to work until he was crawling, it was still valuable bonding time. She also explained, "The great thing, as a working mom, is that you know your baby is taken care of—I don't have to worry about someone else raising my kid."

Mary Admasian said that one reason that Zutano has a baby program is that the company feels that:

> Because [many women are] often given only a six-week period to bond with our young children, it's really important as a nation and as a culture that we support our families in a way that is inclusive.

The critical importance of bonding and secure attachment for babies' development and long-term psychological health is becoming very clear in recent years. Babies-at-work programs make it far easier for babies and their working parents to establish healthy attachment relationships.

## Better Financial Stability and More Options

Being able to bring their babies to work makes mothers much more likely to return to their jobs. Single-income families these days often have made large financial sacrifices (or even gone into debt) so that one parent could stay home with the children, which can harm the stability of the family and the ability of parents to provide for their children the way they want to. But if a mother can keep her baby with her, especially during those crucial first few months, she is much more likely to feel comfortable working at least part time and thus continue to contribute to the financial stability of her family. If baby programs (and programs involving older children) are implemented in our society on a large scale, it is very likely that the number of women feeling compelled to completely leave the workforce will diminish. Since these mothers will be able to wait until their babies reach a level of self-sufficiency before finding other arrangements, they will be able to make a more careful decision about whether to remain employed.

Baby programs can also make a tremendous difference in the lives of single parents and those in lower income ranges. These programs can help parents to avoid the grueling choice between having time with their young babies and having the money to support them. All too many families these days make traumatic decisions in their attempt to give their babies the best life they can. Parenting-at-work programs enable parents to give their children time *and* financial stability.

## Lower Daycare Costs

Parents incur lower daycare expenses by taking their babies to work. For many parents, daycare fees wipe out a significant part of their income and, when commute time and other working expenses are factored in, some parents start to feel as though they're working so that they can pay for daycare so that they can go to work (and this is actually the case for some). On top of this, many daycare facilities have a limited number of enrollment slots for infants under six months of age or don't take babies at all. As Deann Tiede of the Kansas Insurance Department explained:

Infant child care, in particular, is the most
difficult to find and the most costly.
Because parents can bring their babies with
them for the first six months of the infant's
life, it's a tremendous emotional and
financial benefit to them.

Because of babies' tremendous need for dedicated
human contact and social interaction, high-quality daycare
for infants can be difficult to achieve. One study looked at
400 daycare centers in four states and found that only 8% of
the infant programs were of good or excellent quality and
an appalling 40% of the programs were of poor quality.
Sadly, these numbers appear to be similar around the
country.

When a mother has to return to work at four, eight, or
even twelve weeks after her baby's birth, it is very difficult
for parents to experiment with a variety of daycare options
and to find an situation that provides the kind of care they
want for their baby. A baby program allows parents who
plan to continue working outside the home to take their
time looking for the right daycare arrangement for their
baby, interviewing providers, and gradually getting their
baby used to daycare to make certain there is a good fit.

## More Responsive Care Means Healthier Babies

As mentioned, contrary to the often-typical practice in
our culture of waiting before responding to babies (to
"avoid spoiling them"), babies in the workplace have their
needs met quickly, which results in better-adjusted and
happier babies.

Our society is still recovering from the myth that babies can be "spoiled" from this sort of care. This concern raises the question: What does it mean to spoil a child?

Most people consider a child spoiled if he routinely cries or throws a tantrum in order to get what he wants (such as a toy). Older children who do this sort of thing do it because they have found that it works. If parents gently teach children that their behavior is not acceptable, children learn that their tactics are not achieving the goals they seek and they learn more appropriate methods of interacting with other people, such as asking nicely for what they want. However, this dynamic applies *only* to children who are old enough to grasp the difference between socially acceptable and unacceptable behavior and for whom there is a difference between a "want" and a "need." A baby has no means of communicating except through crying, and babies cry *only* when one of their basic needs is not being met.

A baby's needs are pretty straightforward—food, safety, comfort, physical contact, intellectual stimulation, and interaction with other people. They don't cry for "fun" or "exercise" any more than adults cry for exercise, and they don't cry to manipulate other people. When they cry, it is their only way of saying that something is not right in their world—that they're uncomfortable, hungry, craving information, or they want someone to hold them so that they feel safe and secure. Babies don't understand delayed gratification. All they know is that they are hungry now or they are in pain now and the only way they have to ask for help is by crying. Intentionally making them wait before helping them does not teach them patience; all it does is teach them that they need to actually scream (instead of just making quiet sounds of distress) before they can get the help they need.

Babies cry to ask their parents to fix whatever the problem is so that the babies can return to their job of growing and learning about their world. When parents respond immediately to these requests for assistance, the babies learn to trust their parents and their world, and they bond securely with their parents. The babies learn that they are loved and safe and that their parents will be there when they are needed. As they get older, children internalize this belief that the world is a safe, relatively predictable place and that there are people who love them and who can be trusted to help them. These children are thus more willing to venture out and explore the world as they grow up. Children who don't develop strong attachments or who never develop this trust can become insecure as they grow up and can develop other psychological problems.

Although a baby whose cries are repeatedly ignored will sometimes eventually cry less, this method of teaching a baby not to cry can come at a tremendous price. Babies are not born with the capacity to self-soothe. Their brains develop self-soothing mechanisms and patterns from having their psychological and physical needs met consistently and predictably in the first few years of life. More information on this issue is at the Talaris Institute's website (www.Talaris.org/research_aug2006.htm). Babies who are intentionally allowed to "cry it out" are not learning to be independent. They are learning that their parents don't care enough to come to their assistance—or, worse, that they have been abandoned.

The book, *Our Babies, Ourselves*, explains that babies have no conception of the relative safety of modern society. Their self-preservation instincts are rooted in long-term human history in which animal predators were a primary danger. This is another reason that babies are so much happier when they are held or very close to another person (and it's why most babies greatly prefer sleeping close to another person).  Given how helpless babies are, human contact directly represents physical safety and security. Being left alone when they are crying is incredibly scary for a baby given that it suggests that the parents have been harmed or that they have abandoned the baby.  Either possibility, from the baby's perspective, means that the baby is potentially at direct risk of harm from a predator. When babies are left to cry alone for long periods, their brains go into "self-protective" mode.  They ultimately stop crying because there is no point in continuing to call for a caregiver who appears to be gone, especially since continuing to cry (if no one is going to come) increases the chances of the baby being discovered by a predator.

Studies on babies whose cries are repeatedly ignored show that the babies turn inward, become withdrawn, and just stop even trying to interact with those around them.  In the extreme, they can grow up to have great difficulty forming healthy relationships with other adults and with their own children, because they never developed a trusting attachment in those crucial first months of life that determine so much of their perspective of the world.

This is not to suggest that your baby will have lifelong problems if there are a few situations in which you are unable to be with her or immediately meet her needs when she is upset.  Children are very resilient; minor negative experiences are unlikely to have long-lasting effects. However, being as responsive and present for your baby as you can be is ideal for your baby's development and is likely to lead to a happier, more self-sufficient child in the long run.  More information on these issues can be found at the Parenting Counts website run by the Talaris Institute

(www.ParentingCounts.org/Baby_Feel.htm).  When a
baby's needs are met quickly, she does not need to scream
in order to get her needs met; she learns that she is
deserving of love; and she feels that the world is a kind and
welcoming place.  Babies who are raised with this highly-
responsive style of care are often more empathetic and
sensitive to other people's needs as they grow into
toddlerhood and beyond.  This makes sense from a
psychological perspective—adults who feel happy and
secure tend to have a lot more emotional reserves to devote
to caring about and helping other people.

Although some parents in the workplace may be
consistently responsive to their babies primarily to keep
their coworkers happy, this sort of care also directly leads
to well-adjusted and happy children and thus happier and
healthier families.

## Socialized and Happier Babies

Many people in baby-friendly companies commented
that the babies who came to work grew to be unusually
social and independent.  This held true as the babies grew
into preschoolers and older.  Research has shown that
babies who develop a secure bond with parents grow to
have higher self-esteem, be better adjusted, and be more
independent than babies who do not develop a trusting
relationship with their caregivers.  It makes sense that these
work babies, who weren't away from both parents for 8-10
hours a day in those first crucial months, more easily
developed secure bonds.  In addition, since they were
surrounded by many people all day and had lots of adults
interacting with them on a regular basis, these children
became comfortable around many people and learned social

skills as naturally (and sometimes at the same time) as learning to crawl and walk.

Babies learn social cues starting at a very young age, and being around many people on a regular basis gives babies plenty of opportunities to do this. Susan Matthews of Borshoff explained that she felt that:

> [The workplace] is a great environment for babies. They are comfortable with people as a result. They were passed around at staff meetings. They're all bright, happy kids who got to be with their moms for the first six months.

One mother at The Booksource agreed that having a lot going on helped to keep her baby content. As she explained:

> So many people loved to spend time with her during the day. They'd come in and take walks with her, and she'd go visit other offices. I think it was really good for her social acclimatization and was very stimulating for her.

Eileen Hammond noted that, of the babies who came to work at Logan Simpson Design:

> [They] all became very sociable—they would smile at most people in the office [over 60 people]. By coming to work, they were exposed to a lot of people at a very young age and had a ton of people holding them. They spent more awake time at the

office than at home, so interacting with a lot
of people became their frame of reference.

Along with being much more intelligent than many
people realize, babies are also able to sense other people's
moods—and respond appropriately—a lot more than many
people think.  When my younger daughter was just over
one year of age, I was at a friend's house at the same time as
a relative of hers (we had never before met the relative).  A
close family member of the relative had died suddenly just
a few days earlier and the woman was visibly in the throes
of mourning.  She was sitting near where we walked in.  At
that age, my daughter was *very* shy around strangers (now,
at three years old, she enthusiastically says "hi" to everyone
she sees) and would never approach anyone new unless she
had spent extensive time with them first, preferably with
me or her father around.  I was talking briefly with my
friend and noticed that my daughter was intently watching
the clearly distraught woman who seemed lost in her own
world.  To my surprise, suddenly my daughter toddled
straight to the woman and gave her an affectionate hug.  It
was as though she sensed that this woman really needed
someone to comfort her.  My daughter then walked back to
me.  I told her the woman's name and suggested that she go
see her again.  Immediately, my daughter walked back to
the woman and let herself be picked up and cuddled.

Even very young children have tremendous potential to
participate appropriately in social interactions—if we only
give them the chance.  By having lots of people to interact
with and to learn from in babies-at-work programs, babies
become more socially sensitive and aware and fulfill their
stimulation needs at the same time.

# Parents Learn From Coworkers

Many new parents have almost no experience with children before they have their own, and the majority of their knowledge about babies comes from the internet, books, and magazines. Taking their babies to work—instead of primarily being at home alone with them—allows these new parents to benefit from the knowledge and experience of their coworkers. A mother at The Booksource explained that, when she brought her baby to work, a woman she worked with "adores babies and has a magic touch with getting them to sleep. She was able to really help me out with that." The employee explained that she "had a lot of anxiety about being a first-time mom anyway," and that she could "imagine that, if you're on your own and don't have family to come over, it would be very difficult." She said that she was "in some sense relieved to go back to work and be with other adults."

She explained that breastfeeding her baby didn't go very well because she "was paranoid that [her baby] wasn't getting enough food." Even though only a tiny percentage of women are biologically unable to produce enough milk for their babies, this mother's concern is very common in our society. With breastfeeding, it is difficult to objectively measure the amount of food a baby is getting, as opposed to when you see them drink from a bottle. If a new mother doesn't have supportive, knowledgeable people around to reassure her that her baby is doing just fine, she may not have the confidence she needs to establish a successful breastfeeding relationship with her baby and is more likely to give up. Being able to take babies to work gives parents a community of other people who can offer this support and information, making for healthier and happier babies and mothers.

One woman who brought her baby to work said that, as a result of having babies around, people "talk about parenting things, [such as] the birth process and little things babies are doing." She said that having coworkers to discuss things with is a "great support—especially with a first baby." She said that, for her, her first child was "much harder than I thought it would be. It was nice to have the support of other mothers in the office who had older kids, who had been through it. People were understanding and supportive."

Brent Roper of the NAIC explained that "many hands make light work. If a parent is having a bad day, or a baby is, there are a lot of people willing to help."

Kim Martin of Austin, Texas, said that,

> There were days when I would have stuff to get done and the baby needed more attention that day. It was a little bit stressful, but there are lots of women around here who welcomed the chance to walk around with a baby for a bit. I wasn't alone—there were any number of people that had time to babysit for a bit.

This type of social network, in which parents and babies are integrated into society and other people take turns holding and playing with the babies, is how humans cared for children for almost the entire history of our species. As strange as the concept of babies in the workplace might initially sound, it is actually far more natural than isolating new parents and babies the way our society often does.

# Social Network For Parents

Humans are extremely social beings. Yet we expect new mothers to spend the first weeks or months after birth happily alone at home with a baby who requires far more social stimulation than most people can realistically provide on their own.

New parents, especially in the early weeks of their baby's life, often feel isolated and lonely at home all day with their infants while most or all of their friends are at work. Many new mothers joke about how they can't remember how to talk to adults after spending most of their days alone with young children. Taking babies to work provides parents with a strong social support network as well as the assistance of many other people who are eager to play with a baby for a few minutes at a time. Mothers are happier because they are among friends and babies are happier because their needs for human interaction are met. In addition, a happy baby often directly translates to a happy parent.

Kristin Pearson of Health Newsletters Direct discussed the isolation of new parents, explaining that, when her children were born, she stayed home for twelve weeks. As she put it, "man, it was tough." She explained that she did not have family around and, she said, "It would have been extremely helpful to be around other people who could provide insights, advice, and just give adult conversation."

Shannon Cummins of Health Newsletters Direct explained that she had worked for eight years before she had her first child. She was very dedicated to her job and said that she really felt that being able to bring her babies to work was better for her than being home alone with them.

As she explained, "I was never a person who was good at sitting home and doing stuff. You can only clean your apartment so many times." She said that she felt that "getting people back to doing what they find valuable is a big benefit" that comes from baby programs.

JaLynn Copp, who took her baby to work at the Kansas Insurance Department, explained that returning to the social environment of work with her baby definitely helped her mental state. She said:

> I had taken two months off. After one
> month, I was like, 'I gotta get back to work.'
> I love [my baby] to death, but I'm just not
> very domesticated. I was going stir-crazy.
> [My baby] was sleeping all the time—they're
> not really playing at that age—and there's a
> limit to how much TV I could watch.

Sonya Allen of the Office of the State Banking Commissioner in Kansas explained that she felt as though her workplace was "a built-in support network. When you have other people in the office and you're at your wit's end [with your baby], they are willing to take her for a while. If you're home by yourself, it's you and only you." Sonya also thought that her baby benefited by coming to work with her. As Sonya put it:

> Sometimes I think that if you work full time
> and then come home, you're too tired to
> want to do a lot of playing with your child.
> But if you can fit that in, in little bursts
> throughout the day, it makes them happier
> and you happier.

Another mother commented that it's "hard to reach out when you're at home with a brand new baby. I didn't feel inclined to call up people and tell them what an awful time I was having." She said that going to work helped her a lot. "Getting dressed and putting on makeup" to go to work made her "feel like part of the world again."

Sarah Lee of Sarah's Silks worked in Guatemala as a nurse while in the Peace Corps. She explained that, in Guatemala, mothers carry their babies virtually everywhere and just nurse while they're doing their daily tasks, and that it would have been considered extraordinary to hear a screaming baby there. She explained that the women are together nearly all the time as they work; they feel that bonding is very important. She supports bringing babies into the workplace partially because of the social interaction it provides for mothers. As she explained, "it can be very isolating and depressing—and so exhausting— being alone with a baby."

Gay Gaddis, CEO of T3, a marketing firm, mentioned that:

> A lot of different parents have created their
> own community and trade stories. It's like a
> support group in here—especially for the
> first kid. People ease each other's fears.

She explained that some of the women who brought in babies around the same time hired a nanny together since their children already knew each other. She said that having babies in the workplace enabled people to "help solve each other's problems and pass on information."

Nica Waters said that, when her first son was born, she was "living in the middle of nowhere with no neighbors." As she put it, "I went raving bananas." She started bringing her son with her to her job as an administrator at a school when he was only ten days old and she spent time at the school even when she wasn't working. When her daughter was born, she brought her in while she worked. She said, "I would have a hard time being home full time—I figured that out really quickly with my son. I need some other stimulation."

Nica added:

> There's something to be said for the ease with which you can pick a kid up and tend to them, and you realize it's not interfering with work as much as might be thought by someone who hasn't done it. Particularly when they are teeny tiny, which is when moms most need a connection with humans that can talk back to you. I had a tough time with 'eat, sleep, nothing else.' It was just as easy to be at school nursing him as at home nursing, unshowered, and not having human conversations.

This is not to suggest that all parents should take their babies to work instead of staying home with their children if they prefer. Babies-at-work programs simply provide more options from which parents can choose.

## Lower Risk of Postpartum Depression

By being able to delay separation from their babies by bringing them to work, mothers will be at a lower risk of developing postpartum depression. A study of 1,800 mothers found that the longer mothers are able to stay with their babies after birth, the less likely they are to have symptoms of postpartum depression.

The first few months after birth involve extensive hormonal changes in mothers to promote mother-baby bonding. This strong biological urge to be with their babies can make it extremely difficult for a mother to leave her small baby to go to work. Many mothers experience tremendous emotional pain when they must return to work, often due to feelings of guilt and to missing their babies, and the effects of hormones make this even more pronounced. Being able to take their babies to work satisfies mothers' strong emotional and hormonal compulsion to stay with their babies in those early months.

Cross-cultural studies of postpartum depression have found that, across the world, loneliness and "lack of emotional and practical social support" were substantial causes of depression following the birth of a baby. Good social support was universally given as a cause of happiness during this period. Many mothers feel isolated when they are alone at home with their babies all day in those first weeks or months. Boredom is also a problem for many, particularly mothers who enjoyed being productive in their jobs. Being able to bring their babies to work alleviates feelings of isolation, provides mothers with a built-in social network, and provides them with intellectual stimulation that a baby who sleeps fourteen to sixteen hours a day just can't realistically provide.

# Fathers More Involved With Babies

Although our society is becoming more supportive of fathers who want to be closely involved in the care of their infant children, and paternity leave of at least a week or two is slowly becoming more common, there are still cultural obstacles for fathers who want to spend extensive time with their young babies. It used to be believed that babies bonded only with one parent, who generally ended up being the mother due to breastfeeding and due to the fact that the norm was for the mother to spend the majority of time with a new baby. But it is now clear that babies can bond deeply with fathers as well (and, in some cases, with other regular caregivers whom they see on a regular basis and with whom they develop trust that the caregiver will quickly and effectively meet their needs).

Though mothers are currently more often the ones utilizing a baby program, an increasing number of fathers are bringing their babies to work—particularly in companies that have long-standing programs. If both parents are fortunate enough to work in businesses with baby programs, they can take turns taking the baby to work. This would give both parents baby-free days to catch up on any work that is difficult to get done with a baby around.

Taking their babies to work can give working fathers the opportunity to learn to multitask with a baby. It will increase their feelings of attachment to their child, enhance their confidence in their own parenting skills (which can lead to more willingness to take on other parenting tasks), and enable them to be more active participants in their children's lives.

# More Options for Women

In recent years our society has become keenly aware of the growing number of skilled professional women who want children but who postpone having them because they feel that they have to sacrifice either their career or their ability to spend time with and raise their children the way they want to. Many of these women find that, by the time they are at a point in their careers where they feel able to take some time off to have children, their fertility has substantially declined. Even if they are able to get pregnant, pregnancy and birth tend to be more difficult at later ages, and there are higher risks of birth defects. The situation has become an either-or proposition for many—they feel that they can have a successful career or they can have children in their prime fertile years, but not both. For many of these busy career professionals, taking even three months off (and often more) when their babies are born can come at a very high price for their professional reputation and employability. Sylvia Ann Hewlett analyzes this issue in her book *Off-Ramps and On-Ramps: Keeping Talented Women on the Road to Success*, which discusses the costs to women of dropping out of the workforce to raise their children.

The option to bring their babies to work for the first six months or so represents a compromise that can enable more of these professionals to feel comfortable having children before their biological clocks start winding down. It can also help professionals who want to adopt to feel comfortable doing so earlier in life. Bringing their baby to work—and learning how to be productive at work while meeting a baby's needs at the same time—can help parents to find ways to successfully balance work and family life.

One mother explained that to some extent she had identified "her sense of self-worth with [her] success at work." She said that, after being so focused on her job before she had a child, it was hard to find herself "sitting on the couch breastfeeding the baby for the hundredth hour." She said that she really "missed the interaction with other people and feeling productive" in her job. When she brought her children in to work with her at a software company, she carried them in a front pack for most of the day. She said that she only really had to stop working to nurse, since the babies were so happy the rest of the time just being close to her. As she explained, "They don't need anything except to be with you."

Courtney Layton of Austin, Texas, feels that it is beneficial for moms who bring their babies to work to "have other employees to talk to and have that support network." She said that, in her experience, a baby program makes women feel that "it's okay to have kids as a career mom—it makes the women more comfortable and excited to grow their careers."

When professional women forgo having children altogether due to work/life conflicts, society loses the substantial resources these intelligent, educated, and financially stable women have to offer a child (or children). It can also cause tremendous emotional trauma to women in a culture in which being pregnant and giving birth to a child is, for many women, associated with their sense of femininity and self-worth. Babies in the workplace can help alleviate this situation by giving women who want children a way to merge their professional and family lives, and these programs (and parenting-at-work programs involving older children) make it easier for these women to feel comfortable starting a family earlier in life.

Some of the obstacles to professional advancement that mothers face involve the fact that, when mothers take long periods off to stay home with children, they aren't physically present in the workplace. This can result in them not being taken seriously and not being involved in major decisions, simply because they *aren't there* to voice their perspective. Parenting at work minimizes this issue, allowing mothers (and fathers) to raise their children effectively while still being integrally involved in the operations of their organization.

Baby programs also alleviate some of the problems seen in countries with many months of paid maternity leave. Although paid parental leave is fantastic for families and offers benefits for businesses in higher morale and retention of employees, it can be very difficult—particularly for small businesses—to have an employee be gone for such long periods. As a result, businesses in many of these countries are starting to actively avoid employing women of child-bearing age. This also has resulted in businesses questioning women's dedication to their jobs, which diminishes respect for women as professionals. By enabling parents to directly combine parenting with their careers (and by increasing respect for parenting as coworkers bond with children who come to work), parenting-at-work programs provide potential solutions for many of these issues.

Parenting-at-work programs also enable women to have more options for financial independence. A recent book by Leslie Bennetts, *The Feminine Mistake: Are We Giving Up Too Much?*, discusses the risks for women of sacrificing their careers to stay home full time with children while depending on their partners for long-term financial stability.

In this era of high divorce rates and a limited social safety net, baby programs give parents more options for ensuring security for themselves and their families.

| 7 | Top Ten Tips for A Successful Baby Program |
|---|---|
| | **Encourage Breastfeeding** |

# 5

# BENEFITS FOR BUSINESSES

We made [the baby program] public because
we think it's such a great benefit; we share it
with other organizations. At a trade dinner
[in Spring, 2006], our CEO got up and said
[to the other credit union CEOs], "You need
to be doing this."

Wendy Zanotelli, COO
UNCLE Credit Union

## Employees Often Return To Work Earlier

Companies are likely to get new parents back on the job
far sooner with a baby program, since parents don't have to
leave their babies in order to return to work. A company
will thus spend far less on temporary employees or on
overtime for other employees to cover a missing
employee's workload. Parents get to stay with their
children, earn money and maintain their social network and
professional standing, and the work gets done.

As Willie Jones, owner of Magical Journey Bookstore,
explained:

> I got my employee back six times faster than
> I would have. I didn't have to worry about
> covering shifts. It's much easier to stop
> maybe six times a day to cover for an
> employee with a baby than do it all day long.

Fran Oswald raved about how much this factor impacted the branch she manages at Schools Financial:

> It's a dynamite program. I get the employee
> back a lot quicker. When an individual is
> out on maternity leave, under California law,
> I can't replace them. I'm short-handed for
> the whole time. But this way, I get the
> mother back in eight to ten weeks and I have
> coverage again. And the mom is happy
> because she has time to bond with her baby.
> It's a win-win for both employer and
> employee.

Nathan Schmidt corroborated these benefits for Schools Financial, saying:

> The mother comes back to work sooner, so
> we don't necessarily have to direct work
> flow to other employees for as long. It helps
> to facilitate business.

One company allowed a valued female employee to bring in her baby because the employee couldn't afford daycare. It was either let the mother bring in her baby or find a replacement for her. The company's perspective was that, even if the parent got only half the work done, that was still more than if she wasn't there. That parent brought her baby back starting at about 3 weeks after birth, and it worked out well.

Shannon Cummins explained that, when Health Newsletters Direct was still small, they couldn't afford to give employees three months of paid maternity leave. Also, as a result of being small, they "did not have a lot of people who could step in when a parent was out for [even] six weeks with a new baby." Allowing parents to bring their babies to work solved both problems.

Brent Roper said that, before the National Association of Insurance Commissioners implemented its baby program, "Everyone was taking twelve weeks off. The average now is eight weeks and sometimes only six. People come back sooner."

Some mothers decide to completely quit their jobs when their babies are a few weeks or months old. A mother's perspective often completely changes after she has a baby; after only a week or two, it can seem impossible to remember what life was like without her baby. Many women find it difficult to imagine leaving their baby to return to the job world, especially while their babies are still so tiny and helpless. Mothers are biologically programmed to stay close to their babies during those early months; everything in their being is telling them to hold and nurture this little being. Expecting a mother to happily leave her child for eight to ten hours a day during this extremely sensitive period—when her baby is still waking up multiple times a night, may be exclusively breastfed, and can barely even hold up his head on his own—is a huge burden to place on a human being. Cindy Prifti of Shrewsbury, Massachusetts, returned to work when her son was three months old, but, as she explains:

> About two weeks before I had to leave him, I
> started crying every day in anticipation of
> the "big day." I was horribly depressed
> when I was at work, I called [the daycare
> provider] every 30 minutes, and I cried all
> day long.

This scenario is not unusual, especially for first-time mothers, when they must leave their babies in those early months.

Dana Croy of Magical Journey worked in retail for years before she had her own child, and she commented that:

> One of the things that struck me when
> working with women that had babies was
> how unhappy they were when they came
> back to work. I saw several instances where
> women would come back to work and be
> miserable and cry every day for weeks. They
> didn't understand that it was because of
> separation from their baby—the hormonal
> part of it. We have hormones to encourage
> us to take care of babies. Separation messes
> with that.

Dana believes that postpartum depression is often connected to mothers being separated from their babies. She said, "It's against nature. You may be functioning at work, but your mind's not there."

Carolyn Gable, the owner of New Age Transportation, took her twins to the office with her when they were babies. Carolyn explained that part of the reason she started the baby program at New Age is that:

> I know what it's like being a mom,
> especially working an eight-hour day. It was
> easier for me to know that at least [my
> babies] were in the same building as me. I
> wanted to give that opportunity to other
> women.

Melanie Lastra sees huge benefits for Schools Financial from its baby program:

> If [Schools] didn't offer a program like this,
> [these moms] may not return [to work] at all.
> They may be making the decision at home
> without having the advantage of seeing how
> it would work to be working and having a
> baby too. I would think [baby programs]
> would decrease the number of women
> dropping out of the workforce.

Our society considers it crucial to the physical and psychological health of puppies and kittens that they stay with their mothers until they're weaned, generally at six to eight weeks old. These animals can *run* at four or five weeks old, as opposed to a human baby that often goes to daycare before she can even sit up on her own. We separate human babies and mothers at incredibly early ages and then we expect these mothers to be able to focus on their jobs while dealing with the strong biological compulsion to be close to their babies. Allowing mothers to be with their babies at work for at least the first six months keeps them together until the mothers' hormones stabilize and the babies are starting to be independent.

Kandace Bozarth, from Schools Financial, said about her baby:

It was so much better that I was able to bring
her until she was six months old. It was
easier to leave her when [she] was already
crawling and able to do things on her own. I
felt like I didn't need to help her quite as
much, as opposed to if she was only six
weeks old.

Putting a six-month-old in daycare is a far different
proposition than even a two-month-old, especially if the
mother has had her baby with her and been able to bond
and more easily breastfeed for all those extra months.
Kandace also commented that:

I wished I could bring [my baby] longer, but
it was so much better leaving her now than
before. At six weeks, she still wanted to be
held. But now [at six months], she wants to
go and do her own thing. She's more
independent.

Gay Gaddis of T3 thinks that, "allowing babies in the
workplace is worth it even though [the parents] are a little
less productive." She explained that:

For us to replace a person because they
aren't satisfied with their child care
arrangements, it would cost 30% of their
salary to find someone new, and their history
on accounts can be irreplaceable. But being
a little less productive for a few months
evens out in the end.

Bringing her baby to work gives a mother the chance to
get back into the routine of her job. She is able to

experience the satisfaction of being intellectually productive, of interacting on a professional level with other adults, and of contributing to the financial stability of her family.

As Melanie Lastra, a supervisor at Schools Financial, puts it:

> It gives a mother that extra time to be able to think about what she is going to do and to make more educated decisions. She's pretty wrapped up with her baby for the first three months. In the extra three months of bringing her baby to work, she gets to look at both pictures, and a lot of women realize that they can do this—that this can work. It gives them time to breathe and realize they don't need to alter their life drastically right away.

By the time babies are six months old, they're likely to be sleeping in longer stretches at night, so mothers aren't as exhausted as in earlier months. Also, by this time mothers are better adjusted to the idea of being a parent and in more of a regular routine with their babies. Because babies can start having solid foods at six months, breastfeeding moms may not need to pump quite as much milk to keep the baby supplied during daycare, which alleviates stress for moms. In addition, by this time a mother's hormones have stabilized substantially. Mothers of six-month-old babies are in a more grounded frame of mind for making big decisions such as whether to stay employed.

Fran Oswald credits Schools Financial's baby program with the fact that she was able to retain several key employees. As she put it:

> We might have lost some employees if they were not able to be with their babies for the first six months and had that bonding opportunity. We might have had one or two moms decide to stay home. But we retained them by letting them be with the baby for that nursing and bonding time.

Kristin Pearson of Health Newsletters Direct said that:

> My guess is that women who are on the fence about returning to work after having a baby are more likely to return if given the opportunity to bring the baby with them through those important first few weeks.

Deann Tiede, of the Kansas Insurance Department, also felt that the baby program helped some mothers decide to remain at their jobs. She said:

> If you're a first time parent, you may be debating how does one manage all of this. It can be intimidating. [Bringing the baby to work] affords a trial period. The six months is a good demonstration to a parent that they can juggle both family and work obligations. If that's a positive experience, it might suggest to them, hey, I can successfully manage this.

Sally Rynne said that she was never sure whether the mothers who brought in their babies to Health Newsletters Direct would decide to be full time moms when it was time for the babies to stop coming to work. In fact, she noticed the opposite effect. The women were engrossed in their work and glad to return to it without the added care of the baby in the office. She thinks it is "brutal for a mother to be home full time with her baby and then totally separated." Sally also commented that bringing the baby to work provided a "transition period; it was a much easier transition for people that wanted to and needed to work." Wendy Zanotelli said that she definitely believes that their baby program helps UNCLE Credit Union to keep employees. She said that:

> I do not have hard numbers to support that [belief], but I definitely hear employees say, "This is so wonderful. If UNCLE didn't have the program, I might have had to quit my job and stay home because daycare is so expensive."

Daycare, especially for babies, can be so expensive that it takes up nearly all of one parent's paycheck. Being able to bring a baby to work thus allows people who enjoy their jobs to continue to work without sacrificing their time with their babies or their entire income to pay for daycare. Some women who quit their jobs soon after the birth of their babies discover a few months later that they miss the intellectual stimulation and social aspects of going to work, and many families experience a drastically reduced quality of life when they try to make ends meet with a single income. But often, by the time all of the costs associated with leaving the workforce become clear to a mother, her former employer has already found a replacement. These women are then trapped in a situation in which they must spend large amounts of time and energy trying to find a new job while dealing (often on their own during the day) with the challenges of a new baby. Some can't afford to pay for daycare while they look for work, so their efforts are made even more complicated as they try to keep their baby happy while they search for jobs, work on their resumes, and set up interviews.

At the same time, their former employers have usually incurred tremendous costs in recruiting and training a new employee. It is estimated that it costs approximately 30% of a person's annual salary for a company to replace them. Businesses incur costs in searching for and interviewing prospective employees, in unavoidable down time as a new person is learning the job, in lost productivity as other employees spend time orienting and training the newcomer, and in the loss of the experience and industry knowledge of the former employee.

Sometimes parents do decide to stay home full time with their children in spite of the transitional effect of a baby program. But a baby program can have a positive impact on the eventual result of that decision as well. In recent years, as the cost of renting office space has increased and as technology has improved, more companies are allowing employees to work from home. Once a company has seen firsthand that a particular employee can be productive while simultaneously caring for a child, the company is more likely to trust the employee to work remotely while she is at home with her children. Dana Croy and Magical Journey Bookstore found this to be an ideal solution when Dana ultimately decided to stay home full time after bringing her baby to work for several months. Willie Jones, the owner of the bookstore, didn't want to completely lose the benefit of Dana's knowledge about the business, and Dana didn't want to completely lose her income, so Dana began working remotely as a part-time events coordinator for Magical Journey.

In those situations where an employee does decide to stay home after bringing their baby to work, a baby program offers companies and valued employees opportunities to find flexible alternatives. Also, a baby program is an extremely low-cost way for large numbers of companies to experiment with and come to understand the business benefits that come from efforts to help employees balance their work and family lives. A baby program can often be merely the first step for many companies in implementing other measures that make employees' lives easier and benefit the business at the same time.

## Higher Employee Loyalty and Retention

We no longer live in an economic climate in which people expect to spend their entire lives working for the same company. With the widespread use of the internet, talented people can easily network, search for, and apply for jobs in many industries and parts of the country. As mentioned earlier, turnover costs for companies are extremely high, especially in competitive industries. However, for many companies—especially in today's economy—extravagant benefits packages to induce employees to stay just aren't a feasible budget option. Unfortunately, the initial costs of providing on-site daycare (which involve setting aside dedicated space, finding and paying high-quality caregivers, handling changing supply and demand issues since it's often difficult to predict how many children will be in the facility at a given time, and dealing with liability insurance and regulatory issues) make this option intimidating for many small and medium-size businesses. Only approximately 10% of large companies provide their employees with on-site or near-site care, and only about 5% of all companies provide this option.

A baby program provides companies with an extremely low-cost perk that can build very strong employee loyalty, particularly among working mothers. Increased morale is part of the reason that loyalty improves; if people feel happy and content when they're at work, they're much more likely to stay with their company. A baby program also improves people's perceptions of their employer's commitment to its employees, which can be a strong motivation for staying at a company.

Debbie Butler, of Valley Credit Union, commented about Valley's baby policy:

> A lot of employees say that the reason
> they're here is they think it's great that we
> offer that kind of benefit to others even
> though they don't take advantage of it. The
> fact that we offer it is really important to
> them.

Nathan Schmidt said about Schools Financial's baby program:

> [It is a] retention-type benefit to the company
> as well as the employees. Employees note
> the importance of the benefit and that the
> Credit Union understands the needs of
> mothers and employees in the 21st Century.
> Especially in Sacramento, we have very
> expensive home prices, and people usually

need a dual income to purchase a house here.
We recognize this in our economy and this
gives employees an option to have a family
and still afford a nice quality life.

Kelly Howard of Schools Financial said:

Other employers would benefit from
implementing [baby programs] into a
business because it definitely creates a
certain amount of loyalty in employees when
they're given the opportunity to bring in a
baby. [Schools Financial] went that far
above and beyond to let parents be able to
bond with their child in the early stages of
life.

The other people in a work environment also play a part
in whether someone stays with a particular company. If
you like the people you work with and you look forward to
seeing them on a daily basis, you're much more likely to
stay where you are. Knowing that they'll be able to see and
play with happy babies when they go to work can be a
substantial motivation for other employees to stay with a
company.

Though some people's lives revolve around what they
do in their jobs, for many people a job is simply a means to
an end. They may enjoy what they do and they enjoy
spending time with the people they work with but, to a
large degree, a job is something they do primarily for
money, and then they go home to their families and their
"real" lives. When a company understands this and finds
ways to show that it recognizes the importance of family

life to its employees, employee gratitude and loyalty to the company is often extremely strong.

Debbie Butler of Valley Credit Union said that:

> [We've] had moms or dads who brought their
> first and second children through the
> program; they're still working here. They
> say the reason they stay is because they've
> been allowed to do that.

Roxanne Conlin, of the law firm Roxanne Conlin & Associates, explained, "I am positive that our nearly zero turnover is directly related to the flexibility with which we approach this and other matters."

Giving parents the chance to spend those first precious, irreplaceable months with their baby engenders loyalty far beyond most other employee perks. Not only do these programs clearly show a company's commitment to its employees' family lives, but they also directly save employees money since they don't have to pay for daycare and their babies get sick less frequently due to easier breastfeeding and lower exposure to germs than if they were in daycare. The best part, from a company's perspective, is that this retention tool (when structured well) involves minimal cost and minimal disruption to the company, in addition to all of the other benefits that baby programs bring to businesses.

Dana Croy of Magical Journey conceded that:

> Having a baby is a distraction at work. But
> at least it makes you want to be there, and
> makes you really want to do your best for

your employer because they're bending over backwards for you.

Carolyn Gable of New Age Transportation summed up this phenomenon:

> I can go out and get a Fortune 50 company as a client. That is not a problem. My problem is finding good employees who care about customers—employees who care about the freight, about a shipment that has to get there by 5:00 a.m. If I show my employees that I care about them and their life, they, in turn, care about my customers and about New Age.

Deann Tiede of the Kansas Insurance Department said that she has noticed the impact of the baby program on employee retention and loyalty. She said that many of the parents who utilize the program are highly trained and know their jobs well. She said, "If we are able to retain qualified, skilled workers, we will realize an economic savings for the agency."

Audrey Russo of MAYA Design said that, after they first allowed an employee to bring in her baby, "People started to appreciate the perks they get from working here—things they might have taken for granted. Having a baby come in really made them aware of the other perks" the company provided.

Cathy Weatherford of the National Association of Insurance Commissioners explained that:

We had an expectation that we would never
get 100% out of a staff member returning
with an infant.  But in the long run, you end
up with much higher employee retention and
overall good will.

## Increased Morale

All of the businesses with babies-at-work programs
believe that they improve the morale of nearly everyone
around the babies.  The most obvious effect is seen in the
parents who are able to bring their children to work with
them.  These parents rave about how much they appreciate
the opportunity.  Angel Rimbault, of Schools Financial,
commented that the program "was an awesome thing.  It
was wonderful not having to leave my baby with a daycare
person.  Having to do that would tear me apart."  She said:

One of the main reasons I chose to work at
Schools Financial was that I knew about
their policy about babies [in the workplace].
I knew I wanted another child, and that's
why I went to work for them.

Kandace Bozarth, also of Schools Financial, said that,
"It was a great program; I loved it.  It made life so much
easier for me."  Carolyn Gable commented that the parents
who brought in their babies at New Age were "so
grateful—it had a big effect on productivity.  They were so
happy, and they want the best for the company at the same
time."  Carolyn also pointed out, "If I can tell a new mom
to bring her baby to work, it doesn't cost me a dime—and it
benefits everyone."  She also commented that bringing
babies to work is "the best of both worlds."

Jackie Hockaday is a production manager at a marketing firm in Texas and brought her baby to work with her. She explained:

> I have a pretty heavy workload. I was
> worried if I would be able to do it, but I think
> that, as a mother, you're a multitasker to
> begin with. It hasn't been a problem at all.
> I'm actually busier now than before I had
> [my son], but I'm able to keep up with it.
> I'm able to focus on work because I'm not
> worried about my baby.

Cathy Weatherford at the NAIC explained her perspective that:

> So many young parents want balance in their
> life. They want their families, and they want
> to bond with their young baby. But they
> don't want to sacrifice their career or a
> special project at work during that time.

Even if employees have no intention or opportunity to bring in their own children, just having babies around can frequently make people happier. Susan Matthews commented about Borshoff's baby program:

> [It is] such a morale boost. The parents who
> use the program love it. And everyone on
> staff loves having little ones around. It's
> very uplifting. And it doesn't distract from
> doing excellent work for our clients.

As Mark Tatara of Health Newsletters Direct put it, "It's not every day that you're at work and you get to hold and look at a baby." Sandy Jaffe, owner of The Booksource, said that "morale in the company always improved when there was a baby around."

Sally Rynne said that she noticed that the baby program had a major impact on employees feeling connected to and good about working for Health Newsletters Direct. She said:

> Because [the baby program] worked so easily and so well, the people in the company did feel like they were on the forefront of something. They felt like we were different and able to do progressive things. That had a carryover to the confidence with which employees dealt with customers and clients.

Sally explained that there was a "strong sense of identity in the company that we were different and innovative and confident about who we were—and that we could do different things that maybe others didn't do." She said that the baby program "definitely had an effect on the spirit of the company—people were proud of our company and proud of our practices and proud to work in a place that was successful and good."

Sonya Allen explained that, at the Office of the State Banking Commissioner in Kansas, having babies around lightened the mood in the office. She explained that:

> [We] work with bank regulation and numbers—kind of boring stuff. I think it makes it a happier place to come to work if you get to see a baby. Even some of the men I didn't think would have much to do with

> [my daughter] ended up really paying
> attention to her. They wanted to make faces
> at her to get her to smile. Babies are fun!

Wendy Zanotelli of UNCLE Credit Union explained that when one of the employees of the call center wanted to bring her baby, the Call Center Manager had doubts about whether the program could work in a call center environment since a crying baby may be very distracting for a member calling in on the phone. However, she agreed to give it a try, and now Wendy says that:

> [The manager is] one of the biggest
> supporters of the program. She said it did so
> much for the morale of the department. A
> call center environment is high stress
> sometimes, and everyone seems a lot less
> stressed out [because of the babies].

Dr. Mary Secret is a professor at Virginia Commonwealth University who studies parenting in the workplace. She conducted a formal study in one organization with a baby program to look at the reactions of other employees to having babies in the workplace. She discovered that the program had "little, if any, perceived negative effect on the work life of other employees," and that the other employees "expressed overall positive attitudes about the program" regardless of factors such as gender, income, job position, and amount of contact with the babies.

This is not to say that every person in a company loves babies or wants to interact with them. Various companies mentioned that some employees just weren't interested in spending any time with the babies, there were a few employees who thought that babies just didn't belong at work, and there were a few people who found baby babble too distracting. Some companies offer a "baby-free" zone (temporarily moving either the parent or the coworker, whichever option works for all parties) in case particular employees are unhappy being in the vicinity of a baby. Even though employees rarely take companies up on this option, having it available greatly minimizes resistance from employees prior to the implementation of a program. (After implementation of a formal program, most people discover that they love having the happy babies around.)

In many of these companies, the babies actually seem to lower most people's stress levels and defuse difficult situations. As Nathan Schmidt of Schools Financial described, "It helps to put things in perspective when a crisis happens and then you'll start hearing the baby fuss or coo or giggle."

Susan Matthews of Borshoff described having babies around as "uplifting" and that, "If you are having a bad day, you go and get a hug from a baby." Debbie Butler of Valley Credit Union said that in her experience, "Morale is good [from the baby program]. People love having babies around." Angel Rimbault of Schools Financial said, "The other women would come over and say they needed to get their baby fix. They would kiss and hold [my son] for a few minutes, and then go back to work." Willie Jones said that:

> The rest of the staff felt good playing with the baby. They liked being able to share the experience and then be able to walk away.

> It's the grandparent effect. You can enjoy
> the experience with no commitment. It
> brought out the best in everyone.

Lower stress has been clearly linked to better health, which means that these employees are less likely to develop illnesses simply because there are babies around. As Willie explained, being able to play with or hold a happy baby for a few minutes—without having constant responsibility for her—can be incredibly soothing. Kelly Howard, of Schools Financial, commented that:

> Everyone here is really happy and accepting
> of [the baby program]. We all have bonded
> with the babies that have been here. We
> really enjoyed seeing the changes in them,
> when they start becoming really alert and
> smile and recognize you.

Melanie Lastra, who works in the same branch of Schools Financial as Kandace and Angel, mentioned that she actually has a picture of Kandace's baby on her desk. Melanie admitted, "I actually went through withdrawal when [the baby] left." Christine Bierman of Colt Safety commented that babies "bring peace and good energy to the office." Dan Pinger, owner of a public relations firm, explained that:

> [Having babies around is] definitely good for
> morale. A typical business situation is so
> often a harsh world. With the babies around,
> it was a real world. It's not a rough-edged,
> "I'll go to work and I'll make money,"
> grumbling kind of thing. It's a more natural,
> relaxed environment.

Dan Pinger also noticed that "people will ask to hold the baby if they're having a bad day." Kristin Pearson of Health Newsletters Direct noticed this effect as well:

> If someone is in a bad moment—if you've been stuck in front of a spreadsheet for hours or you just hung up the phone from a difficult discussion or were in a tough meeting, you can gain an adjustment on your perspective by being able to walk down the hallway and see a sleeping child—whatever state the child might be in.

Brian Moline described one important meeting he had in his office when he was at the Kansas Insurance Department. He had given his secretary strict instructions not to interrupt the meeting unless it was extremely important. But during a particularly tense moment, he heard a knock at the door. He walked to the door prepared to tell his secretary not to disturb him and discovered instead that the "knock" was from the current office baby pushing her walker against his door, her arms outstretched and clearly wanting to be held. He picked her up and introduced her to the other people in the meeting, and he discovered that her appearance had disarmed everyone and relieved the tension in the room.

Dan Pinger explained that, in his public relations business, a lot of the work was strategic planning on what direction the corporate communications thrust should go, and that it involved a lot of creative thinking. He felt that having babies around helped with this. He said that the babies would often come to internal meetings, and he could

remember people joking, "Ask little Tommy that
question—we can't figure it out." He said that he felt "that
was the kind of thing that took the edge off this being a
business relationship."

Deann Tiede of the Kansas Insurance Department
commented that she thinks the baby program at the Kansas
Insurance Department helps morale. She said that, "I will
pop in on a mom periodically to spend a moment with the
baby and then I'm on my way. A sweet, little smile has a
way of brightening your day." Cathy Weatherford of the
NAIC explained that she's "seen [the baby program] soften
the workplace. Every time we get a newborn, for a couple
of days, everyone rushes to play, touch, and look at them.
But then the baby just becomes a fixture," and people
accept the babies as just part of the environment.

Brent Roper, when asked if other employees complained
about having babies around, gave an example. A married
couple, both of whom work at the NAIC, had recently had
their first child. Brent was talking to the husband and
asked if the couple was planning on splitting their time with
the baby at work so that the baby's presence wouldn't
inconvenience their respective project teams. To Brent's
amusement, the husband said that the decision was actually
a big controversy because their work teams both "wanted to
have the baby all the time."

Jackie Hockaday explained:

> We're driven by some pretty crazy deadlines,
> and people can be stressed out. The minute
> you walk in with a baby, everyone just kind
> of forgets everything, and they relax, they
> talk to the baby, and everyone forgets about

stress for a moment and refocuses. I think
it's refreshing to people. We're all stressed
out, but we have this baby giggling and
laughing and loving life. We reevaluate—
you say, these schedules really aren't that
bad. It sounds silly to say, but that's the
effect.

Wendy Zanotelli, COO of UNCLE Credit Union, said
that:

People pitch in and help out. If a mom is on
the phone or with a member, someone else
will rock the baby or play with or feed [him].
You'll see the CEO or me walking around
with a baby. If people need a stress break,
they go play with the baby.

One mother who brought her baby to work at a software
company said that she thinks that "babies have a very
calming and warming impact on people in general." As she
put it, "People don't want to be energetically negative
around a baby—it's sacrilegious."

Maria Rodriguez of Vanguard Communications
explained that:

[Having babies around] is a stress reliever
for people. Stuff happens—there's pressure
and deadlines. If clients are not happy with
something, it can be really, really stressful.
But if you can walk down the hall and pick
up a baby, you feel better instantaneously. I
can't explain it, but it's just remarkable. If
you're having a bad day—I know other

people have ways they deal with stress; they
take a walk or something. But all you need
to do at Vanguard is walk down the hall to a
baby and you're fine.

## Higher Productivity

Parents involved in the babies-at-work programs at these
companies discovered creative ways to get their work done
in spite of adding "caring for a baby" to their to-do list.
Once most people have a child, they quickly learn how to
get more done during a baby's 20-minute nap than they
ever did during an hour or more of their pre-baby days.
Carolyn Gable said that the saying, "If you want something
done, give it to a busy person," described the parents with
babies at New Age. Deborah Driskill of CDG &
Associates believes that bringing babies actually increased
the productivity of the parents because "[they] aren't
worrying about the baby since the baby is right there.
They're focused and less distracted." She also said that the
parents "became very organized and efficient because they
scheduled their work around the baby's schedule." Nathan
Schmidt said that one of the mothers in the program at
Schools Financial explained to him that:

> The baby gets up when it's time to go to
> work, and gets fed, changed, and dressed and
> goes through the morning routine. He comes
> to work with mom and goes to sleep, wakes
> up around lunchtime, is up for a bit, but then
> goes back to sleep.

Nathan said that what he's seen is that:

> The baby takes on the mother's routine—
> however, a lot of the babies seem to sleep all
> day. After a nap they're alert and up for a
> while, and have their little blanket and little
> toys and are playing—they're not fussy,
> angry, or crying.

Most companies keep employees at their regular pay rate when their babies come to work. The primary companies in which a parent's pay is typically affected during their baby's tenure at work are ones in which employees bill their time. For example, Borshoff typically pays its billing employees at 80% of their regular rate while they have their babies in the office. This is to allow parents to take time to focus on their babies when the babies need attention without the parents feeling guilty about not working during that time. It was also meant to minimize potential feelings of resentment by other employees if a parent was distracted with the baby and not billing as much on a given day. If parents ended up billing at higher than 80% of full time, the company adjusted their pay accordingly.

Several law firms allow babies in the workplace. The legal industry invests a tremendous amount of time and training in new lawyers, which makes retention all the more important (and increases the costs for a firm when a skilled attorney leaves). Baby-friendly firms have found that allowing babies can be invaluable in retaining top female attorneys (and staff) and encouraging women to stay in the profession in general. This is a goal that the legal industry is currently struggling with, as explained in Lauren Stiller Rikleen's book *Ending the Gauntlet: Removing Barriers to Women's Success in the Law*. Because attorneys typically keep detailed track of their time for billing purposes, it may actually be easier for baby programs to become widely accepted in the legal profession (once people overcome any initial skepticism regarding the idea), because law firms are already accustomed to trusting their attorneys' assessment of their own productivity.

All of the law firms with baby programs also allowed non-billing staff to bring their babies to work and, like the other baby-friendly companies with structured programs, they discovered that the parents who brought in babies worked very hard to ensure that they got work done and that their baby wasn't disruptive to other people. These parents understood how much of a privilege it was to be able to keep their babies with them and they were all determined to make it work and to ensure that their company would not feel compelled to change or end the baby program.

Deborah Driskill discussed this phenomenon: "The parents were working a lot harder because they appreciated the opportunity." She also pointed out that, if a first-time parent needed to work a little later some days to catch up on work, it wasn't a problem because, since they had their baby with them, they didn't have to leave early to get to a daycare center before it closed. Nathan Schmidt of Schools Financial said:

> I wish more employers would do it, to create an environment that really puts life into perspective. At first, in certain areas of an organization, it's perceived by people as, "How is this going to impact me?" But it's really not a big deal. The mother gets her work done. It really is a benefit to both the

mother and her family as well as the organization.

Dan Pinger explained, "I think that people with a well-balanced life are far more productive than people who do not have such a balance. This is a part of the balance. And this sort of thing radiates throughout the office." Roxanne Conlin of Roxanne Conlin & Associates commented, "Anything that humanizes the workplace improves productivity and there's nothing more human than a baby."

Mary Admasian of Zutano explained that:

We find that moms want to work more. Because they are given the opportunity to have their baby with them, if they have to take time out for a few minutes [with the baby], they work a little extra or add an hour here and there. It's a nice exchange.

As Fran Oswald, the branch manager at Schools Financial, described:

[The teller mothers] are amazing. I was blown away at how they could do everything one-handed. We have a transaction report that describes how many transactions each teller completes. I compared moms to individuals without a baby. One of our moms was actually completing more transactions on a daily basis than other tellers who didn't have babies to care for!

Carolyn Gable, the CEO of New Age Transportation, made the connection between morale and productivity:

> Babies are pure love. They make people feel
> good. They make people happy. Happy
> people are more productive people. Even if
> they play with the baby for a while, they go
> back and are more productive.

The result of baby programs, in many cases, is that a company becomes more aware of the value of focusing on actual completion of work tasks during the baby's tenure instead of "desk time" as a measure of productivity. Sally Rynne said that, in her experience, having founded a company that grew to employ dozens of employees:

> People can be productive and run rings
> around their job if they want to. And
> probably most people could do their job in
> 80% of the time without much difficulty.
> People gave 110% because they could bring
> in their babies. If they lost some
> productivity during the time the baby was
> there, they gave 110% later.

Parents who bring babies to work quickly find more efficient ways to do their jobs as they learn to effectively combine work and baby care. This benefits the company because parents typically maintain their higher levels of efficiency even after their babies move to another arrangement, which increases the parents' long-term productivity.

Jackie Hockaday feels that she was "much more productive" being able to bring her baby to work with her. She said that she felt like she could "focus on the job knowing he's taken care of." Her baby went to staff meetings, to vendor meetings, and on press checks with her.

She said she felt that having babies in the office creates a "very family-oriented feeling." She said, "It's unbelievable how much work does get done because [parents'] worlds are here while at work and they can be so much more productive."

Jackie added that:

> The weird thing is, I really think I'm more efficient now because I'm so happy in my job right now. It's amazing the loyalty and the respect that [being able to bring in my baby] makes me feel toward my employer.

Of course, every once in a while, there may be a situation in which a parent has difficulty balancing work and caring for their baby or in which a baby at work is unusually fussy. Several baby-friendly companies did say that they could remember one or two babies that were relatively fussy—although often this fussiness was attributable either to the baby having digestive issues from being given formula or to the company not having clear rules about baby crying and parents not immediately responding to their baby's needs. Most of the time, the parent took care of the problem (such as by altering their parenting style or finding a temporary daycare arrangement) without the company having to intervene. However, it is important for companies to have policy provisions in place so that parents understand that bringing in their babies is conditional on the baby's presence not substantially disrupting other employees or preventing work from being completed.

For many parents, minute-to-minute productivity naturally goes down somewhat during the time their baby is in the office. But, as mentioned earlier, parents compensate for this by taking work home, working late as needed, or simply being more focused and productive after their baby has moved to another care arrangement. Also, as Brent Roper of the NAIC points out to his managers, "We're in a tough market. If we can get 70% productivity, we don't have to get a temp, and we don't have to cross-train." He explained, "The babies are only here a short time. We have 20-year employees. What's 3 months in the big picture?"

Mike Griffin of Tucker Griffin Barnes law firm shares this perspective:

> To us it's a fair trade-off—a 30% decline versus not having someone here, or bringing in a temp, or replacing them if they can't come back. A couple of [attorney] partners have said [the baby policy] is what has allowed them to continue to practice law.

Wendy Zanotelli of UNCLE Credit Union said that she thinks:

> [A baby program] makes mom or dad more productive—when another employee is on break, they want to play with the baby. They end up taking over [the baby's] care or doing diaper changing on their breaks, so mom or dad can get more done.

In addition, Wendy said:

> When employees appreciate their employer,
> they are more likely to work harder, as well
> as make suggestions that will increase
> productivity. [UNCLE's] Babies Program
> increases morale and when morale increases,
> productivity increases.

Some of the companies did note a minor impact on the productivity of other employees during the first few days when a new baby came to work. Susan Matthews at Borshoff said that when a new baby comes in, there is a little extra down time as people meet the new person. She said this lasts for only about two days, however, and then, as she put it, other employees, "still ooh and ahh, but while they're working."

Nathan Schmidt said that:

> When a mother first comes back to work,
> people are excited to talk. It's a normal
> human reaction—there's more interest right
> when the baby arrives. That's the only time
> the mother gets less done, because the staff
> is always around the baby.

Nathan also added:

> It was more exciting when the first couple of
> babies arrived, but now it's commonplace—
> you just see babies. The baby becomes part
> of our day-to-day life.

Deann Tiede explained that she was a "skeptic" of the baby program when she began working at the Kansas Insurance Department:

> Our Insurance Commissioner, Sandy Praeger, was very supportive of the program, so I needed to keep an open mind. But to myself I kept thinking, "No work will get done while there's a baby in the office." But as it turned out, that's simply not the case. Yes, people stop to visit the baby from time to time, but overall it has little or no impact on our employees' overall productivity. That's probably the thing that surprised me the most. It only takes a short amount of time and the baby becomes a fixture of the environment—it's not a big thing.

After those first few days of new baby excitement were over, baby-friendly companies found that employee productivity was very high in the baby zones.

There have been a few companies in which allowing babies at work didn't work—but in all of the companies that terminated their baby programs due to problems, there were no prior rules in place to guide people's behavior. There can also be situations in which the requirements of a particular person's job aren't conducive to caring for a baby while working. Catalyst Magazine has had five office babies in the past 15 years. Greta deJong, Catalyst's founder and editor, felt that allowing babies was not the wisest business move in the traditional sense, but she believed that it offered a valuable life experience for everyone. She allowed the babies to come to work because she cared about their parents, believed that babies benefit from staying with their moms, and found that it enriched the office to have the babies present.

Nonetheless, she said that it was sometimes difficult for the parents to effectively do their jobs. Most of the parents who brought babies were in the position of Greta's executive assistant, a job requiring a variety of skills that included running errands, phone work, and meeting with office visitors—activities that a baby often interfered with in the Catalyst office.

With a "village" ethic at play in this office, other staff members pitched in to help out, but Greta relied less and less on her assistant, whose job description became narrower to accommodate the needs of the baby. As the baby neared toddler stage, the parent's stress level usually went up. Then, according to Greta, it would be clear to all that the time had come for some sort of change. Given the specific circumstances involved at the magazine, bringing babies in was not positive from a business perspective and is not an experience she expects to repeat. But Greta emphasized that, on a personal level, she "loved getting to know the babies."

More than 100 organizations have found that the reduced turnover and other benefits as a result of a baby program more than compensate for any short-term reduced productivity of parents caring for a baby while they work. However, the situation at Catalyst Magazine speaks to the importance of businesses planning ways to handle difficulties that may come up and being careful in how a baby program is structured. It is important that businesses be prepared to address concerns with parents and to ensure that work still gets done. Although baby programs have been and can be successful in a wide range of businesses, it helps to set up arrangements in advance to deal with issues. A successful baby program depends on a business being willing to suggest possible solutions to parents, such as asking the parent to set up temporary alternate care arrangements if a baby is unusually fussy for a few days, or bringing a baby to work only a few days each week if a parent needs to catch up on complicated work projects. When businesses plan well and expect the best from their employees, people nearly always live up to those expectations and baby programs work beautifully.

## Lower Health Costs

Although no baby-friendly companies appear to have formally assessed the impact on health insurance costs as a result of their baby programs, baby programs are likely to substantially lower companies' health expenses for a number of reasons. Since, as mentioned, bringing a baby to work makes it much easier for a mother to breastfeed and more likely to nurse longer than if she wasn't able to bring the baby to work, a baby program results in healthier babies. Breastfed babies get sick far less frequently and far less severely than formula-fed babies, in large part due to the targeted antibodies they constantly receive from their mothers while nursing. One key study found that mothers of formula-fed babies took about twice as many days off work to care for sick children as did mothers of breast-fed babies. In addition, child care facilities can often be a breeding ground for antibiotic-resistant germs. By going to work with their parents instead, babies won't be exposed to as many germs in those first several sensitive months.

Kerry Olson explained that, at the North Dakota Department of Health:

[The baby program] was successful for two
reasons. The employees of the divisions are
informed that a baby will be coming to work
and are encouraged to inform their
supervisors of concerns or ideas. Also, the
mothers generally return to work earlier
because they can continue to directly care for
and feed the baby for another four or five
months. It allows them to be more
comfortable because their baby is with them
rather than at a daycare provider.

Parents tend to be more worried about their babies when
their babies are away from them. Bringing babies to work
during those first months lowers stress and provides a
social network for parents, which will make the parents
much less prone to succumbing to illnesses themselves. In
addition, a baby program helps to minimize many of the
stresses commonly associated with having a new baby in
our society. It eliminates or decreases the need to find—
and pay for—good daycare for a very young infant, and it
helps couples to avoid working different schedules to avoid
putting their infant in daycare. It saves new mothers from
the agony of leaving their babies for forty or more hours a
week when their bodies are telling them that the most
important thing is to stay with their babies. All of these
things help to improve employees' family lives and, by
being happier in general, they will be under less stress—
which, again, means fewer illnesses.

Health care costs are also likely to decrease for other
employees in companies with baby programs, due to the
calming effect of holding and playing with happy babies.
People in many companies commented that getting their

daily "baby fix" often made all the difference in relieving stress and tension and helping them feel better about their day.

## Enhanced Employee Recruitment

A baby program also helps to attract skilled employees. Debbie Butler specifically applied to work at Valley Credit Union because she had heard about its baby program, even though her children were all past the age where she could utilize the program herself. She was impressed by the fact that Valley offered such an innovative benefit to its employees and she knew that it was the kind of company for which she wanted to work. She said that she has found that the baby program is very appealing to other potential employees. As she described it, job candidates say, "Wow, I could have brought my baby to work?" Susan Matthews of Borshoff said that:

> We have people coming in to interview for jobs who are single with older kids [and thus wouldn't use the program themselves], but they say, "It's such a cool program, I want to work for a company that does something like that."

Dan Pinger said that:

> [I] think there are people who, when it came to a decision as to whether they would accept our offer to work here or a competitor's offer, they accepted ours. I think [the baby program] was one of the selling points for the agency to get bright talent.

Sally Rynne found that, as clients found out about the baby program at Health Newsletters Direct, a lot of them said to her, "I wish I could work for your company." At the Kansas Insurance Department, they have found that the baby program is very useful for "attracting quality workers." As Deann Tiede explained:

> We're a state government agency. The compensation package may not always be the most attractive. To be competitive, we have to be a bit creative in creating incentives for getting people to want to work here. Those incentives may not come through base salary.

This was a motivation for the National Association of Insurance Commissioners as well. The NAIC President, Cathy Weatherford, explained:

> [When I] came to the NAIC, we started talking about how we could improve the quality of the workplace. As a non-profit, we don't have the ability to play on a level playing field with corporations on pay. We strive for the highest quality of life in the workplace that we could come up with in order to compete.

## Increased Teamwork and Cooperation

Looking for an inexpensive way to enhance cooperation and teamwork at your business? Start a baby program. All of the companies that regularly allow babies reported that having babies at work seems to bring out the maternal and paternal instinct, and cooperative effort, in nearly everyone.

Whenever a mom or dad was too engaged with a customer or other urgent matter to quickly tend to a fussy baby, there was never a shortage of coworkers eager to help. Carolyn Gable of New Age noted that, "What's really nice is that everyone helps each other out. If a mom is on the phone with a customer, both men and women jump up if her baby even squeaks." Nathan Schmidt of Schools Financial pointed out that, "A baby helps to create a team atmosphere." Kelly Howard adds, "Everyone felt very comfortable talking and playing with the babies—it was almost like we all adopted [them]."

Aside from the positive effect that having babies around can have on people's moods, it can also improve people's treatment of each other. Most people instinctively rein in their tempers, minimize their use of negative words, and are generally more pleasant to be around when there are babies or children in the vicinity. Being around babies can bring out the best in people.

Interacting with babies has actually been shown to dramatically reduce tension and aggressive feelings. Roots of Empathy, a Canadian non-profit, brings babies (and their parents) into school classrooms nine times a year so that students can interact with and learn about the babies. Systematic studies have shown tremendous decreases in aggression among students in this program. Interacting with babies makes both children and adults feel calmer and more empathetic toward others—thus resulting in more positive social behavior.

Several companies also noted that, because of the babies, people seemed to talk more about personal issues such as parenting, which gave employees the chance to get to know each other on a deeper level. Willie Jones commented that having the babies around was a learning experience for everyone at Magical Journey Bookstore. He said that both of the mothers who had brought their babies to work were "proactive and constantly talking about different stages of baby development." He said that, as a result, the younger staff members, especially the men and even Willie himself, "became informed about things we might not otherwise have known."

It is rare for many adults—particularly single men—to have the opportunity to be around and to play with a baby for any substantial length of time. Debbie Butler commented that, at Valley Credit Union:

> The men in the organization will actually get
> most attached to the babies. When a baby
> graduates [from the program], it's the men
> who tend to say things like, "I'm really going
> to miss that little guy or little girl." The
> single men say, "I don't hold babies," but
> when the babies come in, they're the ones
> walking around with them. They'll carry the
> baby around. People say things like, "I can
> be having a really sucky day and look over
> and see a cute little baby, and pick her up
> and walk her around for a few minutes, and
> my whole attitude changes."

Melanie Lastra, of Schools Financial, commented on the ability of babies to bring out a new side of people, "People you don't think are that maternal all turn into babbling mothers—everyone ends up getting on their hands and knees to play with the babies."

These baby programs introduced people without children to what babies are really like and gave them the chance to try their hand—even if only for a few minutes a day—at finding the best way to hold a baby and keep her happy. Several people commented on how the quietest and most reserved people in the company often seemed to end up cooing and babbling the most with the babies. Carolyn Gable explained that they once had a young intern working at New Age who was generally very reserved, but who would hold one of the babies on his lap for hours and play with the baby while working at his computer. Having the baby around helped him to open up more with other employees and to develop closer professional connections as a result. Having babies at work allows coworkers to see sides of each other that wouldn't have been revealed without the babies' presence.

By enhancing coworkers' understanding of each other and feelings of closeness, the work atmosphere became a lot more friendly, camaraderie improved and, as a result, people were likely to be much more willing to work as a team. Willie Jones said that there was no resentment from other employees about babies being allowed to come in. He noted that:

> It helped that [the mom] was apologetic if the baby cried; it made people feel better. She never took it for granted. But other staff members actually didn't even need to be asked. If the baby cried, someone would immediately walk over to help.

Alicia Lionberger at Foris Winery said that having children in the workplace "brings a family feel to work—

makes everyone feel that we're all a group, that we're in this together."

Dana Croy at Magical Journey commented that:

> The other employees were great. There were
> several weeks when I needed extra help until
> I was acclimated to being a mom, nursing,
> and working. When orders came in and
> people were needed to receive customers,
> other people would cover the counter for me.
> People helped me a lot. Especially if I
> needed 10 minutes to get [my baby] to sleep,
> I could ask for people to give me some help.

Melanie Lastra confirmed this pattern at Schools Financial:

> The babies were not a disruption for other
> employees. It was kind of a team-building
> thing. It got infectious—everyone pitched
> in. If the baby was getting fussy and the
> mom was busy, we backed up the moms. It
> brought the team effort into play.

Kristin Pearson explained that one thing that she found particularly profound about the baby program at Health Newsletters Direct was how it allowed people to see how "business can be effectively and productively conducted in non-traditional ways—even in the midst of real life going on!" She recalled the company's founder, Sally Rynne, "leading a meeting while holding a fussy baby—patting and soothing while she talked. It was such a sign of leadership strength."

Deann Tiede at the Kansas Insurance Department said that:

> [Having babies around promotes a] true connection between employees. With a baby present in the workplace, many begin to share their own parental experiences with one another. They begin to know even more about one another and that translates to more of a family atmosphere within the work environment. You go from being coworkers to becoming friends and, in some ways, colleagues become an extended family.

Brent Roper of the NAIC explained his perspective:

> When you work with people, politics come into play, people get frustrated, et cetera. But one thing most people can agree on is that you need to treat babies well. It brings people together and softens things up. [Having babies around] tells you what's important in life and what's not.

He said that:

> The relations between employees and managers are very laid-back. There is no question in our minds about the fact that relations between people are being helped by babies being around.

Brent added:

> You can't get 10 people to agree on
> anything—even what color the sky is. But
> when a baby is in the workplace, they are all
> there and very protective. It's a very nice
> thing. It naturally just brings people
> together. You bring a baby in the room and
> people flock there. That was not our
> intent—we were not trying to build teams.
> We were just trying to be good to people at a
> point in their lives when they want to be with
> their families.

Kerry Olson of the North Dakota Department of Health
explained that the baby program created an awareness in
people and got them talking "about the importance of
focusing on family instead of keeping work and home life
separate—as well as the need to promote work-site child
care in North Dakota."

Marie Bevione of Austin, Texas, explained one
interesting effect of having babies in the office where she
worked:

> Babies were good for conversation between
> different departments and were a catalyst for
> people to get to know each other. One of our
> college interns was really good with the
> babies and as a result found himself talking
> with various members of the staff he
> otherwise never would have interacted with.

Wendy Zanotelli of UNCLE Credit Union explained that:

> Everyone is talking more about their
> personal lives [with the babies around]—
> saying things like, "when my son was
> little..." They're getting to know each other
> a lot better.

She thought that having babies around helped with teamwork:

> Even when the babies aren't here some days,
> the morale seems to stay. And even when a
> baby leaves a department, morale does not
> decline—it stays like it was when the baby
> was there.

Wendy said that this appears to be related to the idea that:

> If a parent will entrust a coworker to hold
> their baby when the baby is crying while [the
> parent is] on the phone, that trust level will
> flow over into other things.

Maria Rodriguez of Vanguard Communications said that she has noticed that:

> New bonds get set up. People have said that
> to me. Someone they never had contact
> with—like someone in the accounting
> department who wouldn't interact regularly
> with someone in graphic design—suddenly
> the graphics person comes by to see the baby

and a relationship develops—they now have a bond. In that regard, there's more camaraderie. People will naturally reach out to a person with a baby.

## Attractive To Customers

A baby program can be a great marketing tool for a business. A number of baby-friendly businesses have had their baby programs discussed on the internet, in print articles, or on television. All of the baby-friendly businesses that publicized their programs noticed strongly positive effects on customers' impressions of the company. Since baby programs are still relatively unknown to most of the public, the novelty factor is huge. Companies with these programs report that customers will often come in just to see if the company really does have babies or to visit particular babies to whom they have become attached. All of the businesses in which babies were in public view had customers express sadness when a particular baby reached the limit of the program and was no longer coming to work. These customers missed getting their own "baby fix" and they looked forward to the next baby starting to come to work.

Alicia Lionberger at Foris Winery said that she often had customers come in to check on her baby's progress and that they would be disappointed if he wasn't there that day. She even said that, "People get down on the floor to play with him. No one feels like they have to, but a lot of customers interact with him quite a bit." She said that as a consumer herself:

> It wouldn't bother me a bit to have a salesperson with a baby. I might even be

more inclined to shop there—just because it
looks like a place that supports families.
That's important to me. And it's a place that
obviously cares enough about its employees.

Ted Gerber, the owner of Foris, corroborated Alicia's
impressions, saying that:

[Having children at work is] almost like
entertainment. It gives a "family farm"
aspect to the business—makes it not
corporate. It's like using [the baby] as
advertising or marketing for the winery. It
also adds a warmth that comes through as a
result of having kids around.

Christine Bierman of Colt Safety said that she has never
had a negative comment from customers, and that her
customers see that "we stretch the limits and we'll do
anything we can for our employees."

After implementing a baby program, companies should
easily be able to publicize the program and get at least local
media attention (or national, depending on how large the
company is and how extensive the program is). In recent
months, babies-at-work programs have been discussed in
Time Magazine, People Magazine, and in front-page
articles in USA Today and the Boston Globe, as well as in
dozens of regional newspapers, in international articles, and
on many prominent websites. They have been featured in
television pieces on the Today Show, NBC Nightly News,
Nightline, Fox Business Network, and dozens of local
television news shows, among others. Pieces like these
offer free publicity that helps to advertise the name of the
company to potential customers, along with creating

extremely strong positive associations that will make people feel good about patronizing the business. Babies are pretty much a gold standard for making people feel happy. Sandy Jaffe, owner of The Booksource, explained that, "the baby policy at Booksource has been one of the most successful PR strategies we've developed over the 32 years in business." He said that "the customers loved the policy" and that the policy helped The Booksource to "get and keep employees."

Melanie Lastra said that when Schools Financial first started its program:

> [Schools] really didn't know what the public would think of it. This is a financial institution—it's a different atmosphere than, say, Starbucks. We have a reputation of being professional. But [Schools] thought of [the baby program] as a major breakthrough—to say, "this is what we really want to do for employees."

It turned out, Melanie said, that, "The overwhelming response from customers was positive. They were thrilled and loved it; we got so many comments."

Debbie Butler mentioned that, for six consecutive years, Valley Credit Union was recognized as one of the 50 Best Places to Work in Silicon Valley. She said that one of the reasons it received this honor is because of its babies-at-work program. She said, "People who read that article are very impressed by the program."

For retail or service industries, customers are likely to frequent businesses with baby policies just for the chance to see and play with babies. Also, people with children often feel more comfortable patronizing a business that allows employees to bring their own babies to work. These customers feel as though the business supports customers' families as well as the families of its employees. If a business that caters to walk-in customers doesn't make it easy for parents to come in with their children, those parents are much less likely to come back. Even seemingly little things like not having a diaper-changing table in the bathroom can be a big source of frustration to parents and can be a deterrent to coming to a business. A business that allows its employees to bring in babies is clearly illustrating that it cares about the needs of parents. As a practical matter, it can even make it easier for parents to take their young children shopping or to the bank if they know there will be babies there, since many children find babies fascinating and enjoy interacting with them as much or more than some adults do.

Specialty stores, such as local bookstores, can utilize a baby program to help buffer them from the ever-growing economic threat presented by the internet and large chain stores. To compete with the internet and encourage people to leave their houses to go shopping, some businesses are creating shopping "experiences." People patronize these businesses because they enjoy the ambiance (for example, Starbucks), the novelty (Build-A-Bear stores for kids), or the range of things available for them to do (Apple Retail stores). Implementing a baby program can turn a store into an "experience" for customers, and it actually fulfills all three of these consumer desires. Sleeping or babbling babies transform the ambiance of a business, they have a substantial novelty factor, and they give customers something to do (play with or talk to the baby) while they are on the premises.

Willie Jones, the owner of Magical Journey Bookstore, said that:

> Customers thought it was the coolest thing
> they ever saw. They thought it was great to
> have someone ringing up a sale with a baby
> in a sling on her hip, or a baby laying on the
> hearth asleep in a bassinet.

Dana Croy said that there were many regular customers who knew that her son had been born and who came in just to see him. Magical Journey had discussed her baby in its email newsletter to 8,000 customers, and she knew that some people came in specifically because they had heard about her baby that way. As to the effect this had on the business, she commented that, "especially with a specialty store [like Magical Journey], you can't go in without buying something."

Mike Griffin of Tucker Griffin Barnes commented that their law firm has specifically "gotten clients from [the baby program]. They appreciate what the firm has done and does for people." Kandace Bozarth of Schools Financial said that she never had any negative reactions from credit union members about her baby being with her at the teller window. She said that:

> People commented on how great and family-
> oriented it made the company look. Now
> that Emily is gone [having outgrown the
> program], people constantly want to know
> where she is.

Wendy Zanotelli explained that at UNCLE Credit Union:

> The babies are part of our family now.
> When they come in to the program, they get
> UNCLE Credit Union shirts, with their name
> on the back, the number baby they are in the
> program and a title, and the UNCLE logo on
> the front.

The parents get to choose the baby's title. For example, when the accounting manager brought in her baby, she became the Junior Accounting Manager. One of the babies in the call center was the Call Center Mascot. Although UNCLE is enthusiastic about its baby program, primarily due to how much it benefits employees and the internal business benefits it brings, it probably doesn't hurt its marketing efforts to have its logo being worn by almost 20 babies to date.

## Increased Loyalty From Existing Customers

People want to feel good about the places where they spend their money. An increasing number of companies are donating heavily to charities and social causes because they want to give back to their community and also because it's good for public relations. In this era in which activist analyses and negative customer reviews about a company can be found with a five-second Google search, companies have become much more socially conscious and aware of the importance of soliciting positive publicity about their good deeds.

Implementing a baby program can be a powerful tool for increasing the loyalty of existing customers and for attracting new ones. All of the companies with baby programs whose employees directly interacted with the public found that customers' reactions were overwhelmingly positive. Angel Rimbault, a teller at Schools Financial, said that when she had her baby with her at the teller window:

> It made people have a smile on their face. Women come to the window who are having a bad day and it makes them happier. When they see a baby, it changes their mood.

At Schools Financial, Angel, Kandace Bozarth, and Fran Oswald all noticed credit union members deliberately choosing *longer* teller lines in order to see a baby when they finally reached the teller window. Kandace and Angel both received comments from customers who specifically said that they bank at Schools because they like supporting a company that allows employees to bring their babies. Sandy Jaffe of The Booksource also noticed this effect—he said he has "heard from many people over the years about what a wonderful thing we're doing."

Dana Croy at Magical Journey Bookstore received numerous positive comments from customers as well. She said that was one reason she thought that Willie, the owner, had allowed her to bring in her baby. He had previously allowed another employee, Charity, to bring in her newborn. Dana said that she knew that Willie wanted to meet her needs as a mom and she knew he also really liked getting the positive feedback from customers. She believed that, from the reactions Charity's baby had elicited from customers, Willie saw that letting his employees bring in babies directly helped his business.

Kelly Howard of Schools Financial also noticed very positive reactions. She said that sometimes she would be walking past a teller's window and hear a credit union member make a joke about the baby like, "Don't you think you're starting them a little early?" She said that when she's working with members and they hear a baby making sounds, they often ask what's going on. When she explains, the members "are always pretty amazed by the program and think it's really neat."

Fran Oswald, a branch manager at Schools Financial, said that she has had numerous credit union members stop in to her office—both men and women—to tell her how great they thought it was that Schools offered the baby program for its employees and how they wished they could have brought their babies in at their jobs. She said that she never heard one negative comment from a member. She said that a lot of members actually became sad when a six-month baby period was over and they found out that a particular baby wasn't there anymore. The members wanted to continue watching each baby grow up.

A babies-at-work program also improves customer relations for a more practical reason: people know that they perform better in their own jobs when they are treated well by their employer. When they feel appreciated and happy at work, they have more energy and are motivated to work harder to take care of the company and customers—and they know that other people are the same way. Willie Jones of Magical Journey Bookstore explained that letting his employees bring their babies to work showed that the company was "saying they support you in your life, which I think is an important benefit." He added that it becomes clear that:

> [The company] cares about people as people,
> and the customers see it immediately. It
> doesn't need to be said. If you treat

> employees that way, there's a realistic
> feeling that you probably treat your
> customers better, too.

Having an active baby program shows that a company cares about its employees and doesn't just view them as cogs in a machine. The attitude of virtually everyone in the company—and their interactions with the public—are going to be far better as a result. When members of Valley, Schools Financial, and UNCLE Credit Unions are assisted by a teller whose newborn baby is sleeping contentedly in her lap, they intuitively understand that this happy mother is much less likely to make a mistake with their transaction than if her baby were at daycare and she was distracted due to missing her child or worrying about him.

Kelly Howard of Schools Financial pointed out that, "When credit union members see that the company takes care of employees at that level, they're impressed with the credit union." The customers of these businesses will also extrapolate—at least subconsciously—that if the companies care enough about their employees to let them bring their babies to work, it is likely that the employees are also well taken care of in other ways. They know that employees who are valued by their employers are more dedicated to helping the company and more likely to take extra good care of the company's customers.

As our society has become more mobile and more people are able to work from home, our standards are changing regarding how much time we think people should be able to spend with their families. Companies that can legitimately say they are family-friendly have a significant edge in attracting customers. Willie Jones said that the babies in his bookstore created a "warm, fuzzy atmosphere," and he said that "women wouldn't cross the threshold of the store without making a fuss. Working mothers, especially, liked the idea of being rung up by someone with a baby." He said he got "all kinds of reinforcement that we had made a good decision and that people appreciated it."

Alicia Lionberger said that she frequently would open the door at Foris Winery with her baby in her arms. She found that having her baby with her, "broke the ice. It warmed people up and seemed to give the company more of a home feel."

Wendy Zanotelli said that, when UNCLE Credit Union's facilities person returned to work with her baby, she transferred to the call center during the baby's time at work so as not to have to travel between branches with her child. Wendy explained that credit union members often hear baby sounds over the phone and ask if the employee is working from home. When the mother explains the baby program, Wendy said, "nine out of ten times, [the member] says, 'That's another reason why we love your organization.'"

Wendy said that anyone at UNCLE can bring babies (with the option to temporarily transfer to another position if their primary one isn't appropriate for a baby). Several tellers have brought babies with them and the babies just "hang out" behind the counter. Wendy pointed out that:

> Members love it; they coo at the babies and say things like, "You're so family-friendly. You're already involved in the community, but this drives it home why you're a great organization."

Of course, not everyone approves of babies in the workplace. Several organizations said that they had received a few negative comments over the years from customers who believed that babies were "inappropriate" in a work environment, but that this was more than made up for by the many, many positive comments from people who were enthusiastic supporters of the program. Wendy Zanotelli said that, since 2003, she is aware of only two complaints from members about crying babies. But, she said, she has "lost count of how many positive comments" they have received from customers about the baby program. It is impossible for a business to operate in such a way that its actions please everyone in the public (large corporations are learning this the hard way in this time of well-connected and well-organized activists). None of the companies had even considered terminating their program because of an occasional, isolated complaint. Notably, all of the companies with a baby program that the public knew about said that negative comments were either rare or nonexistent, and they all received a large amount of positive feedback.

## Low Startup and Implementation Costs

A baby program entails very low costs for a company. As mentioned earlier, relatively few companies offer on-site daycare due to the often-high upfront costs such as providing caregivers and purchasing liability insurance. A strong appeal of parenting in the workplace is that the parents retain responsibility for caring for their children, and the company incurs very few costs and minimal liability risks as a result. Parents provide all the toys, blankets, diapers, and other equipment for their babies (although a few companies do provide things like diapers in conjunction with their baby programs).

The only direct costs for most companies are for installing diaper-changing tables if they choose (the most popular ones cost less than $200 each) and, in some cases, paying for an attorney to draw up a legal waiver form for parents to sign. In most companies, there are also incidental costs in terms of time spent by personnel to figure out the parameters of the program.

(The Parenting in the Workplace Institute's website (www.ParentingAtWork.org) offers a free, downloadable, customizable policy for businesses to use that includes legal waiver forms for parents and for alternate care providers, so as to save time for companies and to make this process easier. A "fact sheet" about baby programs is also available, and we will be adding more documentation to the site in the near future for companies to use to enhance the effectiveness of a baby program, such as handouts on baby development, tips for working with a baby, and how to effectively promote a baby program to the public.)

Many companies also temporarily or permanently designate an empty office or break room as a "quiet room" or "family room" for employees who do not have their own offices. Designating a specific area for parents to go is useful for those situations in which a baby is unhappy for more than a few seconds or for private breastfeeding, but it is not an absolute requirement for a successful program. Due to the fact that babies at work are usually so content, these programs have worked well in companies in which employees are in cubicles, in open-plan layouts, and in individual offices (as well as in retail stores).

Once a formal baby program is established, the only ongoing expense for a business is the time spent discussing arrangements with new parents so that they are as effective as possible in their jobs when their baby starts coming to work. Many companies found that it was crucial to discuss ahead of time the nature of projects that parents would be involved in while their babies were in the office, parents' contingency plans if a baby wasn't content at work (although only rarely did these plans need to be used), and who would help watch the baby in the event that a parent couldn't watch the baby for a short time. However, this planning time is substantially offset by the time that a company would otherwise spend finding ways to cover a mother's workload during a lengthy maternity leave, as well as the time and expense involved when mothers decide to quit their jobs rather than separate from their babies in those early months.

Carefully structured baby programs offer extensive benefits for a business at only nominal cost—an impressive combination in our current economy.

| 6 | Top Ten Tips for A Successful Baby Program |
|---|---|
|   | Pre-Plan with Parent |

# 6

# BABIES-AT-WORK PICTURES

More than one thousand babies have been brought to work in baby-friendly organizations. Thanks to the kind permission of several of the participants, here are some of the images that illustrate these programs in action. It is likely that these pictures will become part of a flood of images showing the success of babies-at-work programs.

10-year Babies-at-Work Reunion at Valley Credit Union

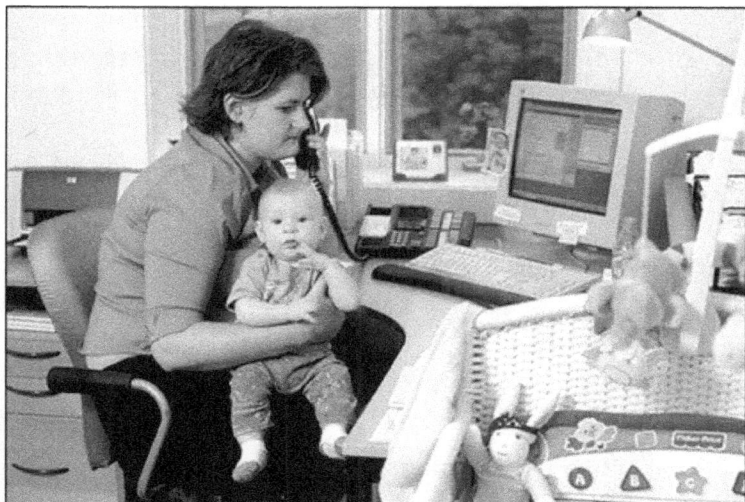
Amanda and Baby Zachary at Zutano

Amber and Baby Carson at Zutano

Angela with Natalie at UNCLE Credit Union

Anne with Krista at Valley Credit Union

Baby Scout with Sherry and Carolyn; Andrea and Allie at Computer at T3

Beth and Baby Hartley at Zutano

Catherine, Amber and Beth, Sales Team at Zutano

Caylee and Mom at the National Association of
Insurance Commissioners

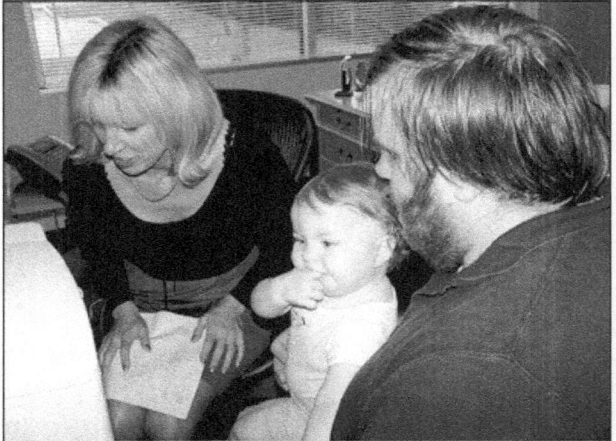

Deborah, Sophia, and Sam at CDG & Associates

Caylee Hanging Out with Mom at the National Association
of Insurance Commissioners

Denise and Baby Lauren at Zutano

Daniel with Isabella at
Valley Credit Union

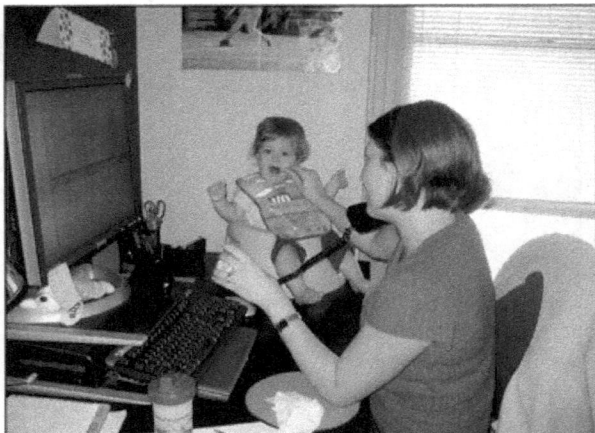

Ellie and Nico at T3

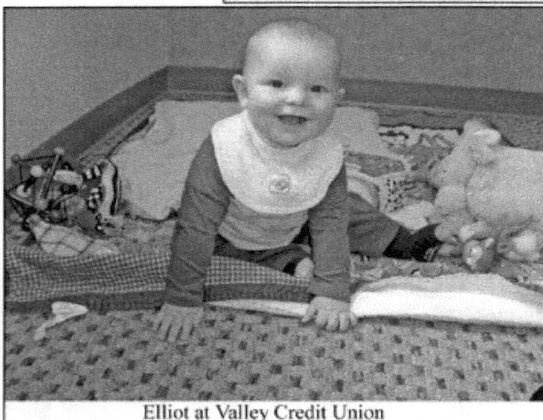

Elliot at Valley Credit Union

Freya at the BLM Office of Fire and Aviation

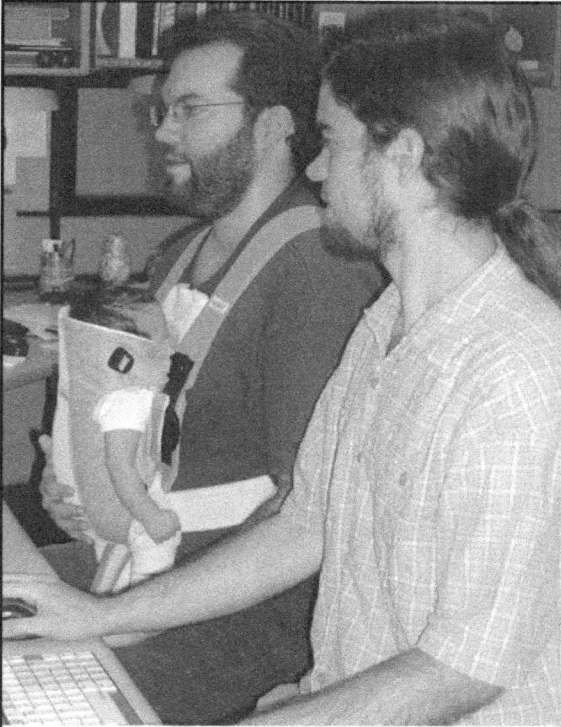

Eric holding Kayla with Matthew
at Ternary Software

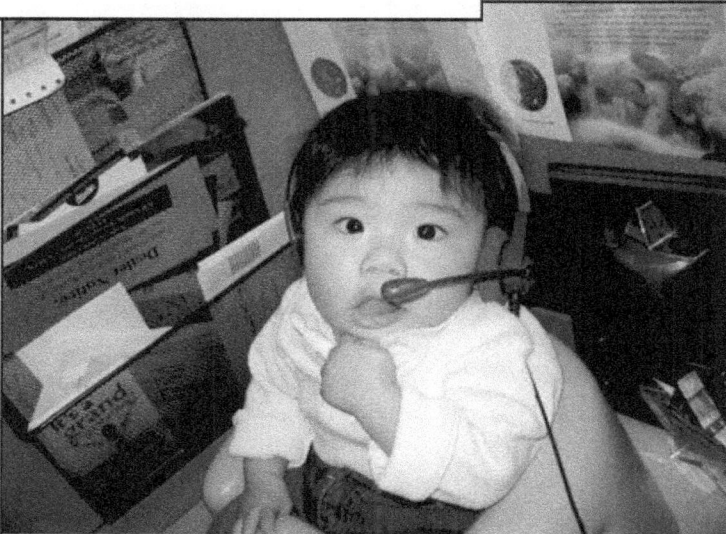

Jaiden at Valley Credit Union

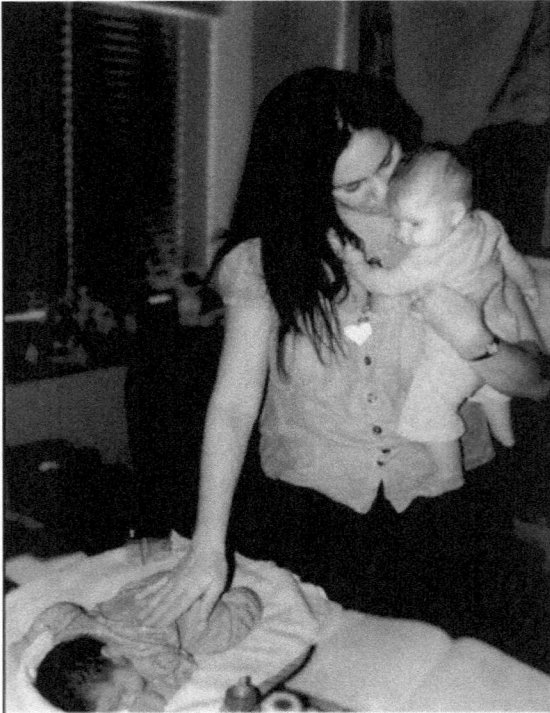

Joy and Babies at PostcardMania

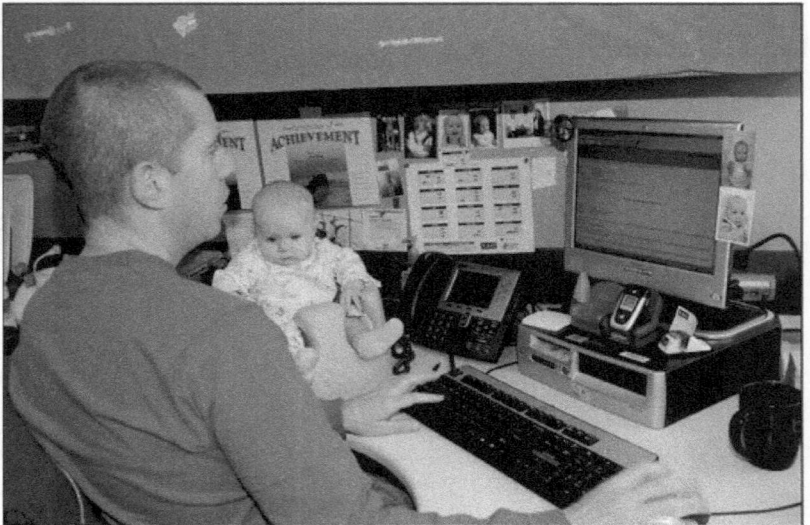

Jon and Baby Jayden at the National Association of Insurance Commissioners

Lyndi and Friends at
the National Association of Insurance Commissioners

Myles with Dollar Dog at UNCLE Credit Union

Ramona and Sophia
at CDG & Associates

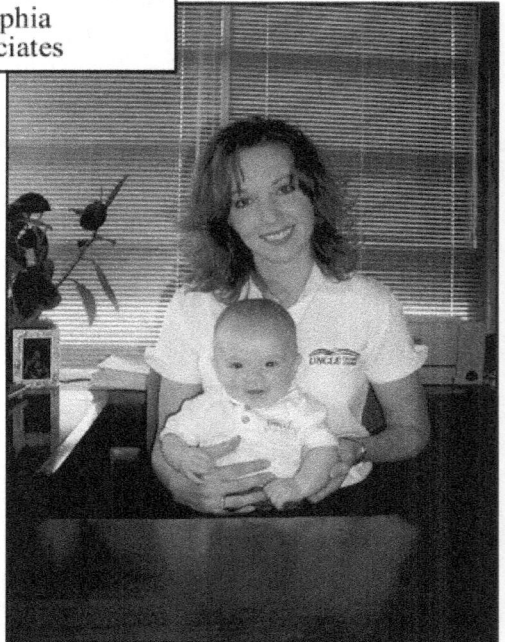

Wendy and Christian at
UNCLE Credit Union

# BENEFITS TO SOCIETY

Having the babies here reinforced to
everyone that we all have a stake in our
children and our future.
>> Willie Jones, Owner
>> Magical Journey Bookstore

## Community Approach To Parenting

Having happy babies in the workplace seems to cause
many people to feel invested in the babies' well-being and
makes them want to participate in getting to know and care
for them. Willie Jones of Magical Journey Bookstore
described that:

> The baby excitement starts when a woman is
> pregnant. When the baby comes, everyone
> wants to crowd around. Even though they're
> not related [to the baby], it really became a
> sense of support and excitement. They
> pretty much act like a family. It seemed a
> natural extension of the phrase, "It takes a
> village to raise a child." Everyone signed on
> to that without ever discussing it. Babies

brought out the maternal and paternal
instinct in everyone, including customers.

Babies are natural charmers—they draw people in.
There's a sentiment among many in our culture—even
before a baby is born—that babies are part of the
community. Many pregnant women have had the
experience of strangers walking up to them and touching
their tummies without even asking first, and the impulse to
touch newborn babies is even stronger. This makes sense
from a biological perspective (even if not from a personal-
space one). Babies are so utterly helpless, and children
require so much dedicated care and attention, that it makes
sense that adults would be "programmed" to instinctively
reach out to children.

This community care is actually a more natural approach
to parenting than our more common arrangement these days
of isolated parents at home alone with children. Having
babies in the workplace results in a social network for
parents, a supportive, caring, and interesting environment
for babies, and a more integrated community.

## Increased Societal Comfort and
## Higher Rates of Breastfeeding

As more babies are breastfed in the workplace and our
society returns to viewing breastfeeding as a normal,
natural part of life, more women are likely to feel
comfortable choosing to nurse their babies (as was the
norm before the extensive marketing campaigns of formula
companies came along).

Mary Admasian of Zutano explained that they actively
try to encourage other companies to implement babies-at-

work programs because they think that breastfeeding is so important for babies and mothers. She said that mothers at Zutano nurse while they're working and sometimes in meetings. Willie Jones of Magical Journey explained how his bookstore's baby program made his employees much more comfortable with the idea of breastfeeding. Magical Journey had a staff room that mothers used when they nursed their babies, but other employees sometimes accidentally walked in on these mothers. Willie said that, in the beginning, the young men who worked at the store would "screech to a stop and turn around" when they walked in on a nursing mother. He said that he discussed the issue with his employees to improve their comfort level, and then, after a while, he realized it was no longer an issue. He said that:

> The third or fourth time people saw [a mother breastfeeding], it might as well have been an elbow. They just got used to it—it was just like any other part of your body.

Due in large part to the aggressive marketing campaigns of formula companies, breastfeeding in public has become relatively rare in our culture (although this is changing, and more states are passing legislation protecting the right of a mother to breastfeed in public). As a result, some people are uncomfortable when they see a nursing baby because they just have no idea how they're supposed to react. Even though women's breasts are specifically designed for the purpose of feeding and nurturing babies and strengthening their immune systems, some in our society consider nursing a baby in public to be inappropriate or even obscene. Our cultural norm is that women's breasts should be covered in public, which actually increases the tendency for breasts to be sexualized (the "forbidden fruit" effect). It is understandably difficult for many people to reconcile the association with sexuality—and society's dictate that breasts are "supposed" to be covered—with the fact that nursing human babies has been the biological norm (since we *are* mammals, after all) since the beginning of humanity.

Another issue that makes some people uncomfortable was described by the editor of a parenting magazine. She pointed out that a mother nursing a baby can be an extremely fascinating thing, especially the idea that a mother's body can actually create everything a baby needs to thrive. It can also be a beautiful thing to watch— especially given how utterly content babies tend to be during and after nursing. Thus, many people are curious about and naturally drawn to look at a nursing mother. But because breasts have become so sexualized in our culture, this creates a mental conflict—people feel as though there's something wrong with them because they want to look, which then makes them uncomfortable with the whole issue.

Interestingly, our culture's discomfort with public breastfeeding is actually more extreme than in some cultures that are far more restrictive about women's bodies in public. A friend of mine grew up in Israel. She remembers regularly seeing Islamic women covered from head to toe in burqas and breastfeeding their babies in public. Interestingly, no one felt that there was anything unusual about this—it was just perceived as being normal and necessary. That starkly contrasts with our culture, where models on billboards and on television often show more skin than the typical nursing mother, but then breastfeeding mothers are sometimes asked to leave public areas when they're discreetly nursing their babies.

Babies-at-work programs, and people's increased comfort with breastfeeding as a result of these programs, can help with all of these issues. As more mothers breastfeed in the workplace (and more mothers are *able* to successfully breastfeed as a result of these programs), people will stop thinking of nursing as being unusual or a novelty. The sexualization effect will start to wear off and nursing will return to being viewed as the natural process that it is—simply a human mother providing human milk to her human child. In recent years, many governments have implemented programs to directly encourage and support breastfeeding to combat the tremendous costs to society from higher mortality rates and increased illnesses when babies are not breastfed. As baby programs are implemented in more companies and breastfeeding returns to being seen as the norm, our society will become more comfortable and supportive of nursing mothers, rates of breastfeeding will increase, health costs will decrease, and everyone will benefit.

## Lower Stress Levels Equal Lower Health Care Costs

If babies-at-work programs become widespread in our society, we are likely to see improved health in our nation as a whole. Babies will be healthier as a result of being breastfed longer. Parents will be healthier due to having lower stress levels during those first months of their baby's life. Other employees in workplaces with babies will have lower stress levels due to the relaxing and enchanting effect of having happy babies around.

Jackie Hockaday said that, in her experience:

> Babies have a calming effect on everyone—
> it puts everyone in a different mindset.
> Everyone warms up and plays with the baby
> and then gets going with a meeting in a good
> mood.

Nica Waters explained that teachers at the school where she worked would ask to hold or play with her baby when they were having a bad day, and that they would comment that a "baby is the best de-stresser around."

Casey O'Connell at the Bureau of Land Management Office of Fire and Aviation described:

> One of the biggest benefits of having a baby
> in the office was the effect it had on other
> workers, most notably my boss. He's the
> head of BLM Fire Operations, and so
> oversees the policy development and safety
> program for approximately 2,000 Bureau
> firefighters, and this job can be incredibly
> stressful. I'd see him return from a meeting
> during the peak of fire season and he'd just
> look beaten down. He'd walk in, sit on the
> floor and goo and gaa at Freya for a few
> minutes, maybe catch a couple of her little
> smiles, and return to the battle totally
> refreshed. It was incredible, and so good for
> both him and her.

Just as many grandparents say that their grandchildren keep them young, having babies in workplaces will go a long way toward improving the health of the people with whom these babies come into contact. In a nation with skyrocketing health care costs, widespread babies-at-work programs could significantly improve the situation.

## People Become Better Parents

By being around babies in the workplace on a regular basis prior to having their own children, prospective parents will feel more comfortable with babies and develop a better sense for how to effectively care for them. Men and women who develop comfort and ease with babies from interacting with them in the workplace are thus likely to be more skilled and confident with their own children. These babies will be less stressed and less fussy, which makes everyone happier.

Babies-at-work programs are also likely to lead to improved parenting. Often, the best way for a new parent to learn effective methods of keeping babies happy is to watch another person interacting with the baby. Babies-at-work programs give parents the opportunity to learn, in an informal way, the techniques that their coworkers use to interact with and entertain babies. These programs also enable coworkers to more easily discuss parenting issues, which will lead to more informed decisions by current and prospective parents. Being out in society with their babies gives parents more opportunities to learn how to make their lives and their babies' lives easier.

Debbie Butler of Valley Credit Union commented that a babies-at-work program is beneficial because:

> It gives people who don't have children the opportunity to see how you can interact and have a job and have children. A lot of times

[other people in the office] think, "no way
could I ever have kids."

However, she said that, after coworkers see parents
successfully taking care of a baby while working, they "find
that you can actually have a life and have children."

A number of people in baby-friendly companies also
mentioned that having babies in the workplace seems to
make non-parents much more comfortable with babies. For
many people, the first time they spend any length of time in
their adult life with babies is when their first child is born.
This can be extremely intimidating for most people and
contributes to the insecurity many parents feel with their
first child. By being around babies at work, people have
the opportunity to learn how to hold and comfort a baby
and they build their own confidence in interacting with
children. Also, considering how deeply many of the single
men at these companies became attached to the babies, it is
entirely possible that, long-term, baby programs could
increase the number of men who decide they want to have
children, as well as potentially increase men's involvement
with their children since they will have more confidence in
their own abilities.

## Societal Change In How
## Babies Are Viewed

Many people in our society still believe that most babies
by nature cry frequently and for long periods of time. As
babies-at-work programs become more common, happy
work babies will help to change this perception. Baby
programs teach people that, if healthy babies are held
frequently, their needs are met promptly, they're primarily
breast-fed (when possible), and they have plenty of social

interaction, they generally cry only minimally—and only enough to attract the attention of someone who will meet their immediate needs.

The contented babies who participated in these babies-at-work programs were not biologically different from other healthy babies. They were just fortunate enough to be in a situation in which they had everything that babies need to be content. As our society comes to understand that these happy workplace babies are *normal*—and that immediately meeting a baby's needs enables her to become healthy and well-adjusted (*not* spoiled)—children, parents, and the rest of society will benefit.

## Socially Integrated Babies

The babies who went to work with their parents tended to be extremely social as toddlers and preschoolers. Humans learn faster during the first six months of life than at any other time. By being taken to work with mom or dad, babies are immersed in a very social environment— they become comfortable being surrounded by and interacting with lots of different people. Although children do interact with other children in daycare settings, the relatively "artificial" environment of daycare provides limited opportunities for children to observe and learn adult interaction techniques and social norms. Baby programs give babies the chance to be exposed to information about how adults interact in the "real world." Being in a work environment during those prime months for absorbing information has a powerful effect on the social awareness and sensitivity of these children throughout their lives, benefiting these children and everyone with whom they ultimately interact.

Debbie Butler commented that:

> [I] think children [in the workplace] become
> accustomed to having other people around
> and are probably more social when it comes
> to having others hold them.

She said that they "respond to people other than their
mother or father." Valley Credit Union has had its program
in place for ten years and she said that the children who
came to work as babies "are very social young children as a
rule." Debbie said, "When they visit, they don't always
remember everyone, but they will say 'hi.' These kids tend
to be smiling and friendly."

Kandace Bozarth commented as to the effect of bringing
her daughter to work at Schools Financial:

> [It] definitely made her so much more social
> and not scared of other people. She's now
> getting to the age where she's a little
> intimidated, but if people smile, she lights up
> and gets all excited. She tries to play with
> people.

Kandace also explained that:

> [My daughter] loves other babies so much.
> She and [another baby] were [at work] at the
> same time, and she was constantly with him.
> She loves being with other people and gets
> along with everyone at daycare. She's been
> there for a month and has had no problems
> adjusting at all.

Alicia Lionberger at Foris Winery explained that her baby "loves coming here; he gets so much attention. There are always new faces, and he enjoys that." She said that he "knows this environment probably as well as his home environment; he's comfortable with it. It's not a huge issue for him to be here." Willie Jones, from Magical Journey, talked about how one of his employees who brought in a baby ended up working part time when her baby was a little older, and how she told him that, "when she was home alone, she wasn't enough for the baby. He had gotten so used to having attention from everyone else!" Given how much stimulation babies crave, this makes perfect sense.

Melanie Lastra went into detail on this phenomenon with the tellers at Schools Financial who brought in their babies:

> One thing that I've seen and heard from moms: they've noticed that the babies are a lot more outgoing—it helps socialization. They get exposed to that kind of stimulation all the time, as opposed to a baby just home with mom who gets codependent with mom and won't let a stranger touch her. They get completely desensitized to new faces and new surroundings and they get more socialized. When they're here, they're right behind the [teller] line with moms, and a lot of times, a mom will have the baby in her lap. The members interact with the babies. They see them, ask about them, and talk to the babies. None of [the babies] are shy. It's amazing. They're used to people coming and going, and used to an active environment and seeing different people all the time. It

may make them mature faster or make them sharper; they seem to be very outgoing as a result.

JaLynn Copp commented that:

> [My child] can really relate to adults because she's around adults a lot—and bringing her to work was the beginning of that. When she went to daycare and saw other kids, she just sat there in fascination for days and just watched. I really think [bringing her to work] helped her grow into being a child that can relate to adults as well as children.

Gay Gaddis said that she noticed a dramatic effect on the work babies at T3:

> Here's a little infant who is exposed to adult conversation every day. If you put them in daycare or at home with the parent, they may be getting some, but I'm convinced that, [because of] the fact that these kids are learning to feel comfortable with others besides their parents, and are listening to adult conversation, that they are picking up vocabulary and speech patterns faster. When they come back to visit, they all seem very mature for their age.

Related to the increased socialization of these babies is the fact that the babies in these programs are exposed to and learn from lots of different people, not just their parents. In addition, all of these people become part of the baby's network. Mark Tatara believes that bringing his son to work at Health Newsletters Direct definitely had an impact on his baby's personality. He said that his son is very friendly, which he attributes to his son "seeing people [at work] smiling at him, as well as seeing them every day." He added that he thinks that, now that his son is older, it almost seems like one or two people isn't enough for him— that "he doesn't see enough people."

This fits with the nature of children and people in general. Humans are extremely social. If we look at long-term human development and the community structures in our history, it makes sense that babies and older children would thrive when they have the opportunity to interact with and learn from lots of different people.

## More Balanced Gender Roles

Bringing babies to work can also help to narrow the shrinking-but-still-present gender gap in the workplace. Our society has come a long way toward accepting that women and men can contribute equally (depending, of course, on their individual skills) in virtually every profession. But, due to the still-prevalent assumption that women are the "natural" caregivers for children, many women are still at a disadvantage for advancement in their chosen fields. Except in the companies that have parenting-at-work programs or other flexible work arrangements, many mothers feel compelled to drop out of the workforce for at least a few months and often for several years after they have children. This "off-ramping" can come at a tremendous cost to a woman's financial stability and long-term career options.

Our culture has finally come to the point of encouraging fathers to be involved with their children; the image of the macho, distant father is no longer prevalent in society. But since the majority of fathers still work full time outside of the home, spending long hours away from home remains an impediment to fathers really spending large quantities of time with (and bonding with) their babies. But the growing babies-at-work trend will help change this. Giving fathers the option to bring their babies to work gives them the chance to overcome their own insecurities and develop confidence in their ability to care for an infant for an extended period of time. As fathers become more experienced and comfortable with caring for their babies— and discover how much fun and how rewarding parenting often is—our culture is likely to change to accommodate men's (and women's) desire to really be active participants in their children's lives.

As more men become involved in their infant children's lives, the cultural assumption that men are "lesser-skilled" caregivers will also diminish. Although our society has come a long way in its view of men as involved, competent parents, we still have progress to make. Mark Tatara said that, when he brought his son to work, "There were a couple of instances where, because I was a man, I was given the 'Oh, let me show you how to do that' routine," even though he had everything well under control.

Mark also commented that his son still treats him as the primary caregiver at times, which Mark attributes to the bond he developed with his son from bringing him to work. Mark explained that, since he and his wife had their second child, Mark is now primarily responsible for his older son while his wife focuses more on the baby.

Babies-at-work programs will increase men's involvement with their children. Although our society is gradually becoming more supportive of men being equal partners in their children's lives, the typical pattern is still that many men spend much of their time focusing on their jobs, and women—even women who work full time out of the house—do most of the child-rearing tasks. Being able to bring their babies to work will give men the chance to actively merge their careers and their family lives and to bond more strongly with their children. It will also help our society to more clearly accept the idea that both men and women are important in nurturing and caring for children and contributing to the community in other ways.

Babies-at-work programs often result in parents receiving *more* respect from coworkers because parents are able to effectively complete their work tasks while also raising a happy, healthy child. This phenomenon, as well as the increasing numbers of men bringing their babies to work, has the potential to increase options for both men and women in the professional world as well as to increase society's support of parenting efforts in general.

## People Open Up Around Babies

Having babies out in society gives people opportunities to express the more nurturing aspects of their personalities. Christine Bierman of Colt Safety explained that her company's customer base is industrial and male-dominated. She said that she's found that the men are "the ones that comment on the babies." She said that many of their clients are firefighters, and that you normally might stereotype them as "tough guys." But, she said, "they're the softest softies in the world—the sweetest and most family-oriented." She said she's been amazed many times to "see this whole other side of them."

Jackie Hockaday confirmed this, explaining that "even the biggest, burliest guys will start babytalking and grabbing baby cheeks. It's just a nice feeling—a family feeling."

## Other People Experience Joy of Babies

Babies-at-work programs offer opportunities for more people to enjoy the calming and rejuvenating effect of being around happy babies. Kerry Olson said that there is no shortage of people at the North Dakota Department of Health to help parents out. He said that, often, "People taking breaks will offer to take the baby for a ride in the stroller. It gives the baby a little room and gives mom some free time." Courtney Layton of Austin, Texas, said that having babies in the workplace is useful for exposing non-parents to the fun of having children. She said:

> For those who hadn't considered having children or who had never spent much time around them, having the babies in the workplace was often eye-opening and inspiring.

Maria Rodriguez of Vanguard Communications said that, when employees choose to have their baby go to daycare instead of bringing the baby to work, they get questions from other employees about it. She said that:

> Employees want the baby to be there. They love having a baby around. Usually folks are chomping at the bit to take care of the baby while [her parent goes] to a meeting.

## Bridges the Gap Between
## Parents and Non-Parents

Having babies in the workplace can help non-parents and parents to more easily relate to each other. Gay Gaddis, CEO of T3, explained that:

> [Having babies in the workplace] has created an understanding for people who don't have kids about how hard it can be to be a parent. People appreciate each other more. Some people don't ever get exposed to parents and babies; it helps coworkers to understand each other's perspective and what they have to deal with.

She explained that one of her reasons for allowing babies to come to work at T3 (a marketing agency) is that:

> [I] look at life in this business as a family on a farm. You know the saying "it takes a village to raise a child"; our ancestors were doing this in a different way. They were working, someone had the baby, someone got the hay in, someone milked the cows, and people tossed the kids between themselves. Here, it takes an agency to raise a child. We help people get through different phases in their lives.

Baby-friendly companies have found that increased communication about people's family situations leads to increased empathy between coworkers, thus leading to better understanding and support of people's individual situations (whether they have children or not). Since coworkers frequently bond with the babies, for many people a babies-at-work program brings into focus the importance of taking care of children—which could have widespread positive ramifications in terms of social policy related to children's health and well-being.

| 5 | Top Ten Tips for A Successful Baby Program |
|---|---|
|   | Babies Can't Be Disruptive |

# 8

# IMPLEMENTATION

## Office and Retail Jobs

Although baby programs have been successful in a wide range of industries, most of the organizations with active baby programs are office or cubicle-based, and several retail stores also regularly allow babies. In some companies, there may be positions that lend themselves to bringing babies and others in which babies clearly aren't appropriate. For example, a worker pouring steel in a foundry obviously couldn't have a baby present, but an office worker in the same company might.

Some companies temporarily move prospective parents to a different position to allow them to bring their baby to work. Debbie Butler of Valley Credit Union explained that she thinks it's important to "have flexibility in people's work hours." She said that companies need to figure out what an employee "can do if they can't do their regular job—what else can they do." She said that Valley is big on cross-training, so that:

> If someone was in a public branch with their baby and it wasn't working, if they were

cross-trained for the call center, they could maybe work there for a period of time.

When asked what businesses were appropriate for baby programs, Wendy Zanotelli replied:

> It's funny—if I had had an interview prior to implementing [the program at UNCLE Credit Union], I would have said not in a bank or credit union. But I now think every bank and credit union should have this program. I think it would work in any business aside from where it may pose a safety issue or if the parent is in a very active job. Even in a retail environment, it could probably work.

In fact, there are at least nine retail stores that have current and successful babies-at-work programs. Having a baby in a retail environment requires more attention to issues related to babies in a public environment and rules related to customer interaction with the babies. However, if a retail employer sets up a clear policy (and ensures that safety is taken into consideration in planning), baby programs can work very well in these organizations (and they have strong benefits in terms of attracting and retaining customers, as described earlier).

## Detailed Procedures and Expectations

Although an informal arrangement has worked for some small companies, there are a number of benefits to having a clear written policy delineating the parameters of a baby program. Angel Rimbault, a mother from Schools Financial, thought it was very important to have a "very specific, black and white agreement saying what could and could not be done." She said that, for example, Schools' policy makes it clear that credit union members are not allowed to hold the babies. She said that, as a parent, she didn't want to walk into this kind of program not knowing the rules. Having a written policy helps make parents more comfortable bringing in their babies.

Brent Roper said that, when they first planned to implement a baby program at the National Association of Insurance Commissioners, "three of my top managers—all women—came into my office and said, 'Brent, you've gone too far with this baby program.'" Cathy Weatherford, the NAIC's CEO, had previously brought her daughter to work at another organization so Brent "knew it could be done," but he said that his managers "even convinced [him] for a minute." So, just in case, when they wrote up the policy for the baby program, Brent said, "we wrote PILOT at the top of the policy so we could end it if it didn't work." But, as in more than 100 other organizations, Brent said that the NAIC discovered that "it was fun, it was easy, and it worked." As of June 2008, 78 babies had successfully come to work at the NAIC.

Susan Matthews of Borshoff explained that if a baby did cry a lot, then it wouldn't work for them to come to work regularly. She said that one of the babies in Borshoff's program cried more than the others, but this was only true very near the end of the baby's time coming into the office, so it wasn't a substantial problem. She said, though, that "companies need to be sure they provide a good work environment for all employees and take care of clients."

While baby programs are generally extremely beneficial and successful, situations may occasionally arise where companies need to be willing to intervene to resolve a situation. This is where it becomes important to have clear rules in place to expedite solving the problem in a well-reasoned and fair manner.

## Expect a Transition Period

Companies should also understand that there will be at least a short transition period during which people get used to the idea of having babies in the workplace and parents get used to balancing their baby and work responsibilities. Most baby-friendly companies said that, when a parent first brought a baby to work, it often seemed to take a week or two for the parent to establish an effective system of taking care of the baby while getting work done. Kandace Bozarth, a teller at Schools Financial, echoed the experiences of several other parents who have brought in babies:

> The first couple of days with [my daughter], I was skeptical it would work. I was totally worn out juggling the baby plus work. But then it became routine and became too easy. She was so good about it!

After this transitional period, the great majority of babies—and parents—in these programs settled into a stable and happy rhythm. Having patience for several days will pay large dividends to the business in the long run.

## Must Be Sustainable For the Organization (It Won't Work For Some Jobs and Some Babies)

Companies should make clear when they first implement a baby program, as well as in any documentation signed by a parent who wants to participate, that the program is conditional on the parent being able to complete her work and on the baby being relatively content such that others in the workplace are not hindered in getting their work done. Even though the majority of babies who come to work are likely to be very content and quiet (for reasons described earlier), there are going to be rare situations in which a particular baby will be too fussy or too restless for them to be able to remain in the work environment. There will also be times when individual parents aren't able to effectively balance their job tasks and caring for a baby.

Although Willie Jones of Magical Journey thought that allowing babies to come in was very successful for his business, he said that companies "need to qualify it—if a child has health challenges, is in pain, or is crying a lot, it won't work. It needs to be a reasonably healthy baby." He said that, if you have a situation where the parent or another person can "get to the baby in a minute to take care of a problem and the crying stops, then it works."

Companies can try to accommodate unusually fussy work babies by temporarily giving the parent an office with a door, if one is available. Parents whose babies cry a lot are likely to feel uncomfortable bringing the baby in anyway, so, in the majority of cases, parents are likely to take the initiative to find other arrangements for the baby if the situation doesn't resolve in a few days.

Businesses should keep in mind the transition period described earlier—that it may take a week or so after a new baby first comes in for the baby and parent to adjust to the routine and the environment. Companies should also take into account the fact that sometimes babies have bad days—perhaps because of digestion problems, teething, or other temporary factors. One option for dealing with this situation may be, after waiting a day or two to see if it resolves on its own, to ask the parent to find daycare, with the option to bring the baby back a few days or weeks later when she is more content. It can be useful if parents have a temporary office with a door they can shut if the baby does cry for more than a few seconds or if the parent wants some privacy.

In many companies, parents were in cubicles or spent time in different places throughout the day in the course of their jobs. Some companies were able to temporarily provide parents with their own offices during the time the baby was coming in. Other companies found it beneficial to designate a room for parents to go to if they wanted privacy for nursing (or pumping), to give their baby some quiet time, or to take a baby who was unusually fussy on a given day.

Parents are going to be grateful to their company for implementing a baby program at all, and the great majority of parents will take action on their own initiative if their baby is disrupting the work environment or if the parent is unable to successfully balance baby care with completing their own work. However, there may be rare situations in which a baby's presence is causing problems but the parent is unable or unwilling to resolve the situation without the company intervening. Making it clear to parents at the outset that the company retains the option to stop allowing the baby to come in will minimize the chances of parents being confused or feeling like they're being treated unfairly, especially if the company explains (and documents, if necessary) the disruptive influence a particular baby has had on the work environment or on the parent's productivity.

Again, this kind of situation is likely to be rare, but having this provision in a baby policy will help improve the outcome (and minimize the risk of coworkers becoming unhappy) if a problem does occur. It is often beneficial to set up a complaint procedure for coworkers to use in the event of problems. Simply having a complaint system in place often enhances parents' focus on being sensitive to their coworkers, thus minimizing the likelihood of situations arising in which people feel the need to file complaints.

A baby program offers many benefits for businesses, but maintaining a work environment in which everyone is able to concentrate still needs to remain a priority for a business implementing this type of program. Companies should not, however, feel that they need to eliminate an entire baby program because of an occasional problem. By accepting that there are situations in which the program won't work, and being proactive about addressing those situations so that a positive work environment is maintained, baby programs are highly likely to be successful in the long term.

## Parent Is Primary Caregiver

It is very helpful for companies to specify that parents are to be the main caregivers for their babies. This is to prevent parents from inappropriately asking coworkers to babysit for long periods of time. Some companies also found it useful to make clear that a parent's first responsibility is their baby when they're at work. By explicitly giving parents the freedom to ensure that their baby's needs are met, parents are happier and thus more productive overall. Also, when parents are able to immediately respond to their babies' needs, the babies generally cry very little—which is one of the keys to a successful baby program.

The parents in these businesses bring virtually all of the supplies for their babies. This lowers liability risks (and costs) for businesses and further emphasizes the fact that the parent is taking on the responsibility for keeping the baby safe and happy. Some companies do give little presents to the babies and nearly all make sure that specific diaper changing areas are designated and available but, for the most part, parents are expected to bring what they feel is necessary for their individual child.

In most cases, parents are still expected to handle their regular workload while their baby is at work. Debbie Butler of Valley Credit Union explained that it is the "responsibility of the parent to adequately balance parenting and work duties" and that the "employee is accountable for the same responsibilities as if no baby was there." This helps to minimize the risks of resentment by other coworkers that might occur if a parent wasn't respectful of the situation and spent much of the day focusing solely on the baby (and not working) while still being paid the same as an employee without a baby. It also makes companies more comfortable with the baby program on the whole.

However, many companies acknowledged that, in practice, most parents are probably only about 70% to 80%

as productive during a regular workday while caring for their baby as they would be without the baby. Parents generally make up for this by staying late as needed or taking work home if possible, because parents don't want their coworkers to feel that they aren't doing their jobs or to have the company ask them to stop bringing the baby to work.

Some companies explicitly take into consideration the temporarily-reduced daily productivity of parents and plan for it. Sally Rynne, the founder of Health Newsletters Direct, said that, after the first baby had come in to work, they did an evaluation of the program. They discovered that the mother felt a lot of pressure to perform at 100% even though she often wasn't able to do so given the requirements of her job and her baby's needs. Sally said that, as a result of this, the company clarified that it was "incumbent on the department heads to ascertain what supplementary resources were required for the parent," and the company gave managers the budgetary authority to provide those added resources. As Mark Tatara, the Art Director at Health Newsletters Direct, and a father who brought his own son to work, explained, the idea was that "additional resources would be brought on to supplement the parent's ability to completely do their job." He said that he thought it was important that a company be aware of this potential issue and to ensure that other workers don't feel like they are constantly called upon to take on more work for the people who bring in their babies. Whether a company needs to temporarily re-allocate resources in this way depends on the specific job responsibilities of each parent and the baby's specific needs; in many baby-friendly companies, parents found creative ways to fulfill all of their responsibilities without the company having to take any special action.

All of the companies with baby programs felt that the benefits of baby programs far outweighed having to consider these sorts of issues. As Mike Griffin of Tucker Griffin Barnes explains, "[Allowing babies in the workplace] takes effort but in the long run the pluses far outweigh the negatives."

In general, most new parents quickly learn ways to accomplish tasks more efficiently after they have their children. Christine Bierman at Colt Safety confirmed that parents work very hard to make the program succeed. She said that:

> [I] can't imagine any employee I've had abusing it. They're so respectful and grateful that they'll work harder, because they don't want to see the program go away.

Dan Pinger saw the same thing at his company. As he says:

> If there's one thing about this whole business, it's that the mother is so thrilled to have the freedom of bringing her baby, that she would stand on her head to make sure that all the work is done. As a matter of fact, sometimes I have thought that productivity has increased because they are so conscientious about making this work.

## Work Still Needs To Get Done

Companies may want to include in their baby policies that customer and client satisfaction are of paramount importance and that the company retains the option to make alterations to the program as necessary to ensure that clients are taken care of appropriately. This will help to remind parents to keep their babies content and avoid disturbing other coworkers, as well as help to minimize the risk that other employees might play with the babies too much instead of working. Ted Gerber of Foris Winery commented that he sees "nothing but benefit" to allowing children to come in "as long as it doesn't cause the business to struggle to operate. As long as the children are well-behaved and don't get in the way, it's not a problem."

Susan Matthews at Borshoff recalled that she had one employee who loved babies and wanted to spend a large portion of her day playing with a baby instead of working. Susan said that she reminded the woman that she was at work and she needed to focus on getting her work done. Once she spoke with the woman, there were no further issues with the woman interacting with the babies to the detriment of her work.

Deborah Driskill commented that the biggest problem CDG had with its baby program was that employees "fought over who got to play with the baby during down time." She said that she has had only "positive reactions" to their baby program, and she commented on the "grandparent effect" in which other employees were able to "get all the good times" in playing with the babies. She admitted that there were situations in which they would have an internal meeting and a baby would get too fussy to stay. But she said that it "wasn't a problem—we just dealt with it. The parent would take the baby out or someone else would help." She said that she didn't have a problem with other employees playing with the babies. She said that she believes that, if they "hire well and communicate clearly, it's not an issue. If someone's job performance is suffering, that's an issue, no matter what the reason."

She explained that "five minutes of talking to a baby is not a problem." If companies are open to allowing other employees to spend a few minutes at a time playing with a baby (which frequently substitutes for activities employees might otherwise do during allotted breaks), the business rewards in employee contentment and long-term productivity will more than make up for these short-but-rewarding "baby breaks."

Debbie Butler said that Valley Credit Union discourages "babysitting" by other staff members. She said she knows that "occasionally mom or dad may be on the phone, and the baby is fussing, and someone else might pick up the baby." She didn't see a problem with this sort of thing, but she said that they don't want a situation where a parent says, "Can you watch my kid for three hours while I do this project?" She said that Valley also makes it clear that they are not providing daycare to parents and that the infant needs to stay in and around the parent's work area. She said that parents need to be sensitive to the needs of others and "maintain as close as possible to a normal work routine."

Wendy Zanotelli explained that UNCLE Credit Union has a written provision that the baby is to remain in the primary care of the parent. However, other employees often enjoy helping the parents out with the babies and playing with them, which UNCLE is fine with "as long as it isn't excessive and doesn't interfere with people getting their own work done." Wendy explained that there is a provision in the policy that states that other employees are prohibited from "babysitting" at work. This is just in case excessive playing with babies becomes an issue, so that UNCLE has an official stance to enforce if someone does take advantage of the situation. She doesn't think that there have been any problems from people occasionally helping with the babies. This experience was echoed in the other baby-friendly companies. As long as organizations make clear the parameters and expectations, parents and coworkers behave appropriately (without company intervention) the overwhelmingly majority of the time.

## Limited Time Period— Only Until Baby Is Mobile

Nearly all of the businesses with a current babies-at-work program allow babies to come to work until they're about six months old or when they start to crawl. The reasons for this are that, when babies start to crawl, they're at a higher safety risk in a workplace environment and it is more difficult to adequately supervise and care for a crawling baby while simultaneously getting work done.

Although there are some workplaces that allow children older than this to come to work with their parents every day, the larger companies found that a six or eight-month limitation (or crawling, whichever comes first) worked well. Susan Matthews of Borshoff said that one of the mothers in the baby program commented that at five months and three weeks, she could see that her productivity was dropping as her son became more active. Susan said:

> When they're little, basically all they need is
> to be fed, hugged, loved, changed, and to
> sleep. This allows the parent to care for her
> child and get work done at the same time.
> But when babies get older, they become

more active, and it's more difficult for
parents to care for their children full time
and also be productive at work. That's why
we end the program when the babies reach
six months.

The six or eight-month window also seems to work well
biologically, since the fact that the baby can crawl coincides
with a number of other milestones that make it easier for
parents to be away from their babies. The first six months
of a baby's life are an extremely key time for babies and
parents. In that relatively short period of time, most babies
change from being completely helpless and dependent to
being able to hold objects, interact with their environments
by their own choice, and travel under their own power.

Also, if a breastfeeding mother can bring her baby to
work until six months (when her baby starts being able to
have solid foods) or eight months of age, she will be much
more likely to have established a successful long-term
breastfeeding relationship with her baby. She will also be
more able to maintain a sufficient milk supply after the
baby goes to daycare since her baby will no longer be
completely dependent on her milk. A six-month-old baby
is far more independent than a baby even a month younger
and, as a result, the prospect of a baby of that age being
away from her parents while they're working seems a far
more reasonable proposition to many parents than prior to
that time.

It would be great if all parents had the option of working
with their children until a year of age or longer, but the
mobility limitation is a feasible compromise between the
needs of parents and babies and the needs of businesses.

# Discuss Baby Program
# Prior To Implementation

A company considering starting a baby program may find it useful to solicit feedback from employees prior to implementation and when babies first start to come in. Parents and coworkers are likely to be able to offer valuable suggestions for ways to make a baby program as effective as possible in a particular company.

Willie Jones of Magical Journey Bookstore found that discussing the baby program with all of his employees was highly beneficial. He said that he spoke to the other staff members before he first agreed to let an employee bring in her baby. He said he asked for other people's opinions and made sure they understood that they might need to cover for the employee occasionally while she had the baby there. He believes that they appreciated that he asked for their thoughts on the decision and that the discussion helped prevent people from having issues when a baby actually started coming to work, because they had "bought in" to making it work for the company as well as for the parents. This option is likely to work well in smaller companies with more informal work environments. It can also provide an opportunity to fine-tune the specific provisions of a baby program to the particular needs of a company, its employees, and its customers or clients.

Large companies may find that soliciting input and approval from all employees simply isn't realistic. However, something that worked well for many of the larger companies was discussing the baby policy with those who would be located close to a baby before the baby first arrived in the office, explaining the purpose and parameters of the baby program, and addressing concerns that people had about the baby or about work getting completed. It can also be helpful for management to send a memo or email to all personnel when the baby program is first implemented. The memo could explain the rationale for starting the program, the basic guidelines, and the expected results and benefits, and invite people with specific concerns to share them and make suggestions for improvement as the program gets underway.

In addition to discussing a baby program with employees in the abstract, it can also help for parents to touch base with their immediate coworkers when their baby starts coming to work. MAYA Design is an extremely open, no-walls work environment. Audrey Russo of MAYA said that the first employee to bring in a baby sent a note out the first day she came in with her son, saying, "Hey neighbors, welcome my son and [me]. I know this is going to be an interesting experiment. I want you to tell me, or talk to HR, if anything bothers you." Audrey felt that this was a very valuable part of integrating the baby into the workplace.

In discussing a prospective baby program with employees, it helps for companies to be aware of—and help to correct—the mistaken assumption many people in our society have that all babies by nature cry for long periods. Also, if a company educates its employees about the goals and the positive effects of baby programs and makes it clear that the company is committed to making the program work, employees will be more likely to keep an open mind about the concept and to be flexible about helping to make it work.

# Top-Down Support

Managers, parents, and coworkers all mentioned that having a baby program be supported at the top levels of a company is crucial to its success. Some people believe that babies aren't appropriate in a work environment. Because of this, it helps if a baby program is explained and wholeheartedly supported from the top.

Carolyn Gable of New Age said that, "Once you [have a baby program], you can't imagine why everyone wouldn't want to do it. It's 100% positive—there's no downside to it." She explained, though, that "it has to be in an environment where it works. If I'm a career person and don't like kids, it might not work." She noted how important it is to have upper management supporting the program; she said that it really helps "people [to] buy in to it." This is primarily important in the early stages of a baby program. Once a program has been in place for a while, the positive effects will be seen firsthand by employees and the company culture is highly likely to become very supportive of the baby program for the long term.

# Baby-Free Zones

Some companies found that offering a "baby-free work environment" helped to minimize employee concerns. Offering coworkers the option to have their work area moved or the option to temporarily have the parent and baby move to a different location minimized the risks of resentment or frustration by other employees. None of the profiled companies actually reported resentment by coworkers, but some wanted to make this option available to minimize the risk in the future. Debbie Butler said that employees of Valley Credit Union who are disturbed by an unusually fussy baby can request a temporary transfer to a different area and that Valley will attempt to accommodate them. Schools Financial also has this provision in its policy (but has not yet had anyone ask for an accommodation).

## Designated Alternate Care Providers

Several organizations with baby programs require parents to name two "designated alternate caregivers." These are coworkers who volunteer and explicitly agree (generally in advance of a baby starting to come to work) to watch the baby for a short time if the parent has to attend a meeting or needs to focus completely on a work project for a while. These coworkers sign a form acknowledging their willingness to do occasional baby care (generally limited to a maximum period of time in the course of a day). This gives parents the opportunity to carefully consider which coworkers they want to have directly involved in their baby's care and formalizes these people's role in backing up a parent. The organizations make it clear that these alternative providers are still expected to complete their own work; they can't just babysit all day.

Designating specific alternate caregivers minimizes the risk of people feeling pressured to babysit who really aren't comfortable doing so. Maria Rodriguez of Vanguard Communications explained that one issue she is careful with in her company is that people not ask those they supervise to watch their babies when they need to go to a meeting. She said that she has made it clear that if people ask others to watch their baby, they need to ask someone who doesn't report directly to them. Otherwise, she said, "the employee might feel pressured to do it—they might be concerned about receiving a bad performance review if they didn't take care of the baby, when that has nothing to do with their work."

In all of the baby-friendly companies, most coworkers voluntarily offer to help with the babies for short periods of time. However, designating specific alternate providers is very useful in that it gives parents a clear plan for what to do if they are in an urgent work situation and need a few baby-free minutes. It also greatly minimizes the risk of someone being asked to help with a baby who really isn't comfortable doing so (and thus minimizes potential resentment issues).

## Discuss Details With Prospective Parents

As Kerry Olsen of the North Dakota Department of Health explained, it can be useful—before each baby starts coming to work—to discuss with the parent any issues that might come up. Brent Roper corroborated this view—he said that only once (out of more than 75 babies) was there a problem with a parent bringing in her baby and that it was due to not having problem-solved up front. Some things that companies found valuable to discuss prior to each baby's arrival at work included:

- Areas in which the parent thought they might need extra assistance when their baby was at work

- Logistics (available quiet room, what furniture the parent wanted to bring, what they would do with diapers or other trash, and what they needed in terms of a place to nurse or otherwise feed the baby)

- Whether the employee planned to return to work full time or part time, and how often the employee planned to have the baby with them at work

- Planned method of feeding the infant (explain benefits of breastfeeding)

- Discuss policy and plans during division meeting attended by all division employees—especially any in the general vicinity of a baby

- Whether daycare backup is arranged in the event of an unusually fussy or ill baby

- Parent's current workload and any high-stress or intensive projects that may be coming up in the near future that may need more staff allocated to them while the baby is there

## Costs Of Implementation

The cost of implementing a baby policy is very low. The primary expense incurred by some companies was for the installation of diaper-changing tables in restrooms (approximately $200 per table). If a company wishes to establish a formal "baby room" or "family room," setting up furniture and a lock on the door may require a small expenditure. Once any initial setup is complete, however, there should not be any ongoing direct costs for a company since parents bring their own baby supplies and are directly responsible for the baby's care. (As mentioned, a free template baby policy including legal waiver forms is available from the Parenting in the Workplace Institute for companies to download and customize as desired.)

# Legal Issues

One of the biggest concerns of many companies considering a baby program can be how to handle legal issues and potential liability risks. They may be concerned about the liability of having a baby in a work environment and whether the company is at risk of being sued if something happened to the baby. Many baby-friendly companies dealt with this issue by making it clear that the parent is the primary caretaker for the child and making sure the parent explicitly understands that the company is not accepting responsibility for taking care of the child. Having parents sign a legal waiver form also helps to minimize potential issues by minimizing the company's legal responsibility for the child's well-being. (There are also obvious safety rules—children should not be brought to workplaces in which they would be exposed to dangerous conditions such as weapons or hazardous materials.)

Although there appears to be minimal legal precedent related to parenting in the workplace (likely because these programs work so well in practice), general "public safety" rules appear to be most applicable to a business with a babies-at-work program. Several decision makers at these companies said that, according to their attorney, letting a baby come to work under the care of the parent was like a parent taking a child to a grocery store. Susan Matthews of Borshoff explained that she uses a document written by her attorneys that relieves the company and other employees of liability for the baby. She used the analogy that, if you take your baby to the store, the store has the responsibility not to, for example, let shelving fall onto you or your baby, but they are not responsible for taking care of your baby aside from that sort of thing. In other words, the grocery store is not responsible if a baby gets hurt while a parent is shopping there unless the store is negligent or otherwise responsible for creating a clearly dangerous condition that causes the harm to the child.

This principle is supported by a New York case from 2007 related to children at work. The situation involved a father (who owned a construction company) bringing his six-year-old son to work with him at a construction site. The case discusses whether the construction company itself "owed a duty" to the child as it would to "any other member of the general public." The court in the case found that the company itself had no legal duty to ensure the child's well-being because the father "voluntarily had elected to" take the child to work at the site and it was not at the company's "invitation" (which might have been the case, for example, if the company invited a group of students to tour the facility). There was no suggestion whatsoever that a company might be held to any higher standard than what it would have had toward the general public. The case concluded that the "safety and care [of the child] solely and exclusively befell his father" and that there was no legal duty on the part of the company.

Thus, when parents are explicitly accepting full responsibility for their child's care in the workplace and a company does not take on the responsibility of providing care for the child, a company's potential liability is minimal. Even if a duty were placed on the company, it would in most cases be limited to ensuring that there are no clearly dangerous conditions on the premises. This is something that a responsible business would already be doing for its employees. If crawling babies or walking toddlers are allowed on the premises, this creates different risks for the children and the company (since these children would potentially be at risk from things like computer cords that wouldn't normally present a risk for employees). But setting a not-yet-crawling limitation on the program (as do most companies) goes a long way toward solving this issue.

Higher liability—and insurance—issues come into play when a company sets up an official daycare operation in which the company provides a caregiver for children. Carolyn Gable explained that New Age had provided an on-site babysitter for a time but stopped the practice when her attorney told her that her liability risks were much higher by doing this. Susan Matthews said that Borshoff had also considered having a "baby room" with paid caregivers but decided that the liability risks were just too high.

On-site daycare facilities are a great perk in larger companies that can afford to cover the costs for space, providers, and insurance. But for smaller companies, or even for large companies who are trying to rein in costs in an increasingly difficult economic climate, a babies-at-work program—in which parents are responsible for their own children—can be an ideal start. Brian Moline, the attorney mentioned earlier who worked at the Kansas Insurance Department when its baby program was started, was initially worried about liability but is now a staunch supporter of these programs. He said that, "While lawyers have concerns about things like that, they tend to overreact. My observation was that, while anything can happen, the chances [of problems] were remote." The minimal liability risks of these programs are also illustrated by the fact that several law firms allow babies at work, as does the National Association of Insurance Commissioners. In addition, the Society for Human Resource Management estimates that 29% of businesses allow employees to bring children to work on an occasional basis—thus further indicating that parenting at work is not seen as a major liability concern from a business perspective.

One exception to the generally low liability issues may be if employees are permitted to take their babies with them while they are driving on company business. Although Logan Simpson Design, a landscape architecture and environmental planning firm, is very pleased with its policy of having babies in the workplace, they have a firm rule that employees are not allowed to take their babies into the field with them—even in the parent's own car—while the parent is on company business. Logan Simpson does not want to expose the baby to field conditions or undue risk, nor does it want to risk responsibility for any liability that might arise if the baby were accidentally injured while traveling.

Other companies aren't concerned about this issue since most have parents sign a liability waiver document. Schools Financial Credit Union had a facilities manager who took her baby with her when she traveled to branch locations to oversee construction projects; Schools had no concerns or problems with the arrangement. A number of other companies also have employees who regularly take their babies with them if they need to visit other facilities during the work day. This issue (along with many others) really comes down to what parameters match a particular organization's comfort level.

## Case By Case Basis

For those companies that aren't yet ready to implement a full-fledged baby program, it's possible to try the baby idea on a case-by-case basis (although it is still important to establish basic rules of conduct). Many companies across the country have allowed an employee to bring a baby or older child in on an occasional basis, such as if regular daycare unexpectedly fell through. For example, a mid-sized law firm in Massachusetts allowed Cindy Prifti, a legal secretary, to have her infant son in the office over her lunch hour every day for three months. Her son had started refusing to take a bottle at daycare, so Cindy had her daycare provider bring the baby to her over lunch so that she could nurse him.

Each day, the caregiver would arrive at noon with the baby, Cindy would feed her son in a vacant office, and then she would spend the rest of her lunch hour just wandering the halls of the firm with him while he slept or looked around. Much like the babies in official babies-at-work programs, Cindy's son was extremely content just watching the events of the workplace. To babies, an office environment is quite exciting—there are people walking around, people talking, people laughing, people typing on computers, lots of machines that make interesting sounds, windows to look out of, and plenty of other things to learn about.

## Older Children

Companies may also want to experiment with allowing older children to come in on an occasional basis. An increasing number of companies across the country are allowing older children to come to work on special occasions—such as on school holidays or snow days. (The 29% of companies currently allowing children on an occasional basis is up from only 22% in 2006.) Willie Jones, the owner of Magical Journey Bookstore, mentioned that his son will occasionally spend the day in the bookstore and often he'll just wander around the store and say to each customer, "Welcome to Magical Journey." Dana Croy, who brought her baby to work at Magical Journey, explained that Willie's philosophy was that she could bring her baby "until it wasn't working anymore." She suggested that it is useful for a company to make it clear that they "realize that [the parent] has some needs right now" but that it's not a permanent thing. Using this open-ended concept as a guide, companies could allow parents to bring in their children when they're babies or even when they're older, as long as the children are well-behaved and aren't disruptive from a business standpoint.

Allowing older children at work can add a whole new layer of benefits for businesses. Holly Reigh, the co-owner of Reigh Services, a landscaping and home maintenance business in Centre County, Pennsylvania, discovered this firsthand. Her nearly-three-year-old son, Jameson, had accompanied her to client meetings and job sites from babyhood and thus became very familiar with the basics of the business. One day, Holly was chatting with an acquaintance at the woman's house and, in the middle of the conversation, Holly's son suddenly commented to the woman, "You need mulch." The lady laughed and said, "Oh, really?" The boy replied, matter-of-factly, "Yes, you do, and my daddy can bring you some." The woman was charmed by the child's straightforward attitude and asked Holly what he was talking about. After Holly told her about the business, the woman actually ended up hiring Holly's company to put in mulch.

Although not every company will be fortunate enough to have preschoolers bringing in new customers, the concept of how to integrate older children into the work world is worth further exploration. (The Parenting in the Workplace

Institute plans (as we grow) to do research and analysis on parenting-at-work programs involving older children and to help companies to set up sustainable policies.)

| 4 | Top Ten Tips for A Successful Baby Program |
|---|---|
| | Have Alternate Care Providers |

# 9

# PARENT TIPS

## Responsive Care

Responding immediately and effectively to your baby's needs is an important part of raising a contented and well-adjusted baby, and highly-responsive care makes it much easier to keep a baby happy in a work environment. As you become more confident as a parent and more skilled in discerning what your baby is asking for, you and your baby are likely to develop a happy rhythm. The more quickly you meet your baby's needs, the less time she will need to spend crying to communicate them. This means she has more time for her primary job of learning about her world and you'll have more time and energy for getting work done and playing with your baby.

Providing your baby with lots of affection and responding immediately to her basic needs will make your baby far more content, since she'll quickly learn that she doesn't need to resort to full-out crying to get your attention. Although it may sometimes seem like more work in the short term to respond so quickly to your baby's whimpers, the rewards for you and your baby are immense.

In cultures in which the concept of "spoiling a baby" never affected people's views, parents raise their babies according to their parental instincts and in a way that allows the parents to accomplish their daily tasks as effectively as possible while keeping their babies happy. They hold their babies nearly constantly and keep their babies close even while sleeping, which makes the babies feel safe, comfortable, and secure. Mothers breastfeed according to the babies' desires—not on a "schedule." The babies feel that they are a part of the social world because they are able to see and be part of the social interactions of their parents.

Responding quickly to your baby's cries—from birth—fosters healthy bonding and attachment, which is critical for normal emotional development. Contrary to the "responding too fast will make a baby spoiled" mantra of some in our culture, babies who are given attentive, responsive care are actually far more likely to grow up well-adjusted, emotionally secure, and independent.

When a baby knows that she can trust her parents to be there when she needs them, she develops a sense of safety and security and thus feels more comfortable eagerly exploring her world. One explanation for this is that the baby feels that she has a "secure base" that she knows she can return to as needed—and just knowing she has that trusted parental "base" makes her feel empowered to make her own way. If a baby is left alone for long periods of time or never knows whether her basic needs (for touch, nourishment, love and interaction, and security) will be met, this actually leads to the child becoming far more "clingy" and insecure as she gets older—out of sheer self-preservation. In order for children to thrive, they must have adults they can trust and depend on to meet their needs.

Being highly responsive to your baby will help keep your baby happy and easily calmed and thus make it easier for you to successfully get work tasks done at the same time.

## Breastfeed Your Baby

Breastfeeding is by far the healthiest option for your baby, and it is an incredible method of keeping babies content. Babies have a powerful sucking impulse, which strongly suggests that frequent breastfeeding is the biological norm for babies and that babies breastfeed for more than just food intake. This isn't surprising considering that breastfeeding provides incredible immune system benefits for babies as well as perfect nutrition (even from mothers who aren't eating a perfectly well-balanced diet themselves).

In the workplace, frequently breastfeeding your baby is a great way to keep your baby healthy and content. If your workplace environment supports it, nursing at the same time that you're working can be very effective. Many mothers use a nursing pillow (one of the best-designed and popular brands is a Boppy). The pillow goes around the mother's waist and the baby can nurse while lying on the pillow. Using one of these pillows is a great way to keep your baby happy while allowing you to get work done. (In the early days of my children's lives, I spent many hours working at my computer as my baby nursed while lying on a Boppy or slept nestled against me.) Keeping your baby close generally means she'll sleep more deeply and comfortably because she won't feel the need to frequently wake up to make sure she's still in a safe environment.

If possible, exclusively breastfeeding your baby (not giving them anything except human milk) for the first six months is ideal for a baby's immune and digestive systems. However, *any* amount of breastfeeding is beneficial for your baby. Many working mothers find it difficult to pump enough milk during the day if their baby is in full time daycare, and some quit from the mistaken belief that, since their baby is getting formula at daycare anyway, there is no reason to continue nursing at all. But combining formula and breastfeeding is far better for your baby than not breastfeeding at all. *Every time* your baby breastfeeds, you are strengthening her developing immune system, which provides lifelong benefits as well as providing comfort and nurturing for your baby.

If you are not in a position to breastfeed every time your baby is hungry, you may wish to pump milk for others to give to your baby. If you are able to take your baby to work even part time and nurse frequently when you are with your baby, this will help to maintain your milk supply and make it easier for you to pump enough milk to keep your baby supplied. If a father is taking his baby to work, it is helpful if the mother can pump milk for the father to feed the baby with a bottle. In this case, a bottle or pacifier should not generally be given to the baby at all for about the first four or five weeks of life. If a bottle is introduced earlier than this, it can interfere with the baby's ability to nurse effectively and can hinder long-term breastfeeding (waiting much past this time can sometimes make it more difficult for the baby to get used to a bottle if you plan to introduce one).

A valuable resource for breastfeeding questions is *The Breastfeeding Book: Everything You Need to Know About Nursing Your Child from Birth Through Weaning* by Dr.

William Sears and Martha Sears. The website
www.WorkAndPump.com contains extensive, practical
information for working mothers on pumping, maintaining
a milk supply, and answers to many other questions.
Another great site for breastfeeding information is
www.KellyMom.com. If you need personal assistance with
breastfeeding issues, you can hire a lactation consultant
who will come to your house (for a fee) to help you
directly. La Leche League International is also a great
resource. La Leche is an international breastfeeding
support organization that offers free, 24-hour information
and personal telephone assistance for nursing mothers on
any topic relating to breastfeeding. Local La Leche League
groups also hold regular meetings that provide a social
network for mothers and give detailed information on
breastfeeding and other parenting issues.

Sleeping close to your baby and nursing during the night
can also greatly help to maintain your milk supply, since
prolactin (a nursing hormone designed to create a sense of
calm and well-being in nursing mothers) production is
highest at night. Keeping your baby close during sleep is
actually the biological norm for our species and often
makes it easier to establish a successful breastfeeding
relationship.

Dr. James McKenna is the director of the Mother-Baby
Behavioral Sleep Laboratory at the University of Notre
Dame and has been studying mother-baby sleep for more
than 15 years. He has discovered that, when breastfeeding
mothers and babies sleep close together, their sleep patterns
get into sync. This means that, when the baby is in a light
sleep cycle and starts to wake up, often the mother does too
(sometimes a few seconds before her baby even makes a
sound). The result of this is that when a co-sleeping baby

needs help, her parents generally aren't wrenched out of a deep sleep the way they might be if the baby were crying from another room.  Co-sleeping mothers can often more rapidly soothe their babies (sometimes before the babies are even fully awake), resulting in parents and babies being able to return to sleep much more quickly and easily—and thus get more sleep overall.  Mothers who breastfeed and co-sleep with their babies often don't even remember how many times they woke up during the night, since they frequently wake up just enough to help their barely-awake baby latch on and then fall easily back to sleep while their baby nurses contently back to sleep as well.  This coordination in sleep patterns appears to have a protective effect on infant breathing during sleep.  There is also evidence that sleeping close to your baby and breastfeeding have a protective effect against Sudden Infant Death Syndrome (SIDS).  Many cultures that routinely co-sleep with their infants have much lower SIDS rates than ours.

Our culture is one of the very few in which even very young babies are routinely expected to sleep alone.  Our culture frequently presents solitary sleeping as the "norm" and thus very little information is presented to parents on safe co-sleeping.  The problem with this is that, due to their biology and self-preservation instincts, babies are naturally driven to sleep close to another person—and even many parents in our crib-focused society sense and respond to how much better their babies sleep when they are close to their parents.

A New York Times article from 2003 explained that a National Institute of Child Health and Human Development study found that nearly 50% of infants spent "at least some time sleeping in an adult bed in the previous two weeks."  This is an incredibly high percentage, given that parents are routinely told that crib sleep is inherently safer and that co-sleeping is "maladaptive" (an illogical claim considering that co-sleeping has biological advantages and is the norm in most of the world)—and it just shows how strong our biology is.

For parents who want to utilize the benefits of sleeping close to their babies, Dr. McKenna's book *Sleeping With Your Baby: A Parent's Guide to Cosleeping* is a comprehensive and interesting read that provides extensive information on co-sleeping and how to do it safely. The book explains the data on co-sleeping and gives information on various sleeping options for parents to consider, such as separate "co-sleepers" that attach to the parents' bed. Clear guidelines for how to co-sleep safely can be found at the following location: (www.attachmentparenting.org/support/articles/safesleepgu idelines.php). Co-sleeping has actually been linked to high levels of independence and social competence in later childhood and adulthood.

This is not to suggest that everyone should co-sleep; parents vary in the sleeping arrangements that work best for them. However, if done safely, co-sleeping (or keeping your baby close in a co-sleeper, bassinet, or crib) is a perfectly natural and healthy option for your baby.

## Physical Contact

Babies are born expecting nearly-constant physical contact. Human touch is incredibly important for emotional and physical development and it helps babies to feel safe and secure—which makes them cry less. In a work environment, the more your baby is held (be it in a carrier or just nestled in your lap) and touched, the more content your baby will be. Slings and wrap-style carriers are the best carrier options for promoting proper physical development. One popular option for parenting at work is the Moby Wrap, a wrap-style carrier that allows for discreet nursing and enables you to have your hands free to get tasks done while keeping your baby happy. One major benefit of a wrap like the Moby is that it is highly adjustable—which means that it allows different people to easily carry the baby during the workday.

Too often in our society, we think of holding babies as a "treat" for the baby—as though touch should be rationed. But, to babies, constant physical contact with another person is what they expect and crave. If you think of constant holding as the "norm" (which it is from a biological standpoint) and make your decisions from that perspective, you and your baby's lives are likely to be a lot happier.

Some parents become concerned that they are holding their babies "too much" and that the babies will never become independent. The scientific and biological evidence is clear, though, that frequent holding is crucially important for babies and that babies who develop secure attachments through regular positive contact with their parents grow up to be far more well-adjusted and independent. There is also a myth in our culture that, if you hold your baby too much, she will have trouble learning to crawl and walk. This theory is also not supported by the actual evidence. In fact, extensively carrying a baby in a sling or wrap (particularly in lieu of leaving them on their backs in a stroller or car seat) actually helps with proper muscle development. (Anecdotally, I carried my babies virtually nonstop from birth and they were walking on their own at eight and nine months of age, respectively.)

Keeping your baby close to your body has extensive physical and emotional benefits for your baby and the greater contentment of your baby means an easier and happier life for you as well.

This is not to say that you can't ever put your baby down next to you while she's happily exploring a toy or while you're talking to her. But extensive holding is by far the healthiest approach for your baby. It's also an easy way to increase your own strength, especially in those early months as a new parent when time for exercise is hard to come by. If you start holding your baby regularly when he is just a newborn, your strength and endurance will naturally increase as he grows, with minimal discomfort or extra effort on your part.

## Adult Tools Are Toys To a Baby

Babies are born with a powerful desire to learn. Essentially everything they do is geared toward that goal— including, especially, playing. They explore every aspect of their world so that they can understand it better and handle life as effectively as possible. As a result, babies are fascinated by the activities of other people and they are motivated to experiment with the tools that other people use.

Most parents these days have seen how fascinated babies and toddlers are with telephones. From an early age, children will try to play with their parents' cell phones, push the buttons, and pretend to talk or listen. This sort of thing is how children learn about the world—by watching others, imitating what they see, and experimenting to gather information.

What this means from a practical point of view is that the most effective "toys" you can give your baby while you're trying to work are often the basic tools of daily life. This includes things like a comb, a spare keyboard (these can often be found inexpensively at thrift stores—make sure to remove the cord for safety), a realistic-looking toy cell phone (so your baby doesn't accidentally dial 911, which happens more frequently than you'd think), crumpled office paper, and other things (safe for babies) similar to what your baby sees you using on a regular basis.

## Talk To Baby About Work

Babies crave human interaction. Explaining what you're doing while you work can be a great way to keep your baby content while still getting work done. Place your baby on your lap or close by so she can see your face and your work area, then read memos out loud to your baby as you're proofreading them. Pretend that your baby is a trainee and (quietly) explain the nuances of your daily tasks to her. One side benefit of this is that, as you're describing your daily routines out loud, you may well discover more efficient ways to do regular tasks.

Babies begin learning language before they are even born. Talking to your baby means you are helping her to learn language as well as increasing the bond between you and her. (Not to mention that talking to your baby while you work is a great excuse if you're in the habit of occasionally talking to yourself—you can just claim, "Oh, I was talking to the baby.")

Even in the early months, babies are absorbing information even if they can't always express their understanding at the time. Anne Nolan worked as a judge's clerk until her baby was about five months old and regularly brought her daughter to work with her. When her daughter was about one year old and able to talk, Anne took her daughter back (for the first time in seven months) to visit Anne's previous coworkers. Anne's old office was now being used by someone else. As Anne and her daughter were walking past Anne's former office—which Anne had *not* pointed out to her daughter—the child suddenly took a detour away from her mother and into the office. She walked purposefully to the desk chair, patted it, and said confidently, "Mommy." Anne was delighted that her daughter so clearly remembered the environment where she had spent her early months of life. The reality is that all healthy babies have this sort of memory and intellectual capacity—if we only give them the opportunities to make the most of it.

## Locate Baby For Social Interaction

Another great way to keep babies happy when they're awake is to locate them where they can easily interact with people passing by (while still being close enough to you that they feel safe and secure). Babies are very receptive to social cues and to learning human interaction styles, so frequent interaction with other people is a valuable tool for your baby's development as well as their contentment. This also has the benefit of providing your coworkers with the chance to get to know you and your baby and to become more comfortable with babies in general (which is beneficial for our society as a whole). Having your baby with you at work can be a great conversation starter and can lead to discussions and friendships you might not otherwise have had, so you can build your support network this way as well.

# Locate Babies Near Each Other

A number of parents who brought their babies to work noticed that babies placed close to each other often start cooing at and interacting with each other. If there is more than one baby in your office at a time, try to make the most of this opportunity to let your baby get to know another child (which can also keep your baby happy and give you more dedicated time to get work done).

# Work During Baby's Naps

Babies sleep a lot, especially in the first six months of life. If you are keeping your baby in a sling or other type of carrier, your baby will probably sleep for longer stretches at a time than if they are alone and not in physical contact with another person. Make the most of these nap times. Many parents quickly learn more efficient ways to do work once their babies are born and thus are able to accomplish a tremendous amount in an hour or two of nap time.

# Let Other People Help

Several companies ask parents to designate specific coworkers who are willing to help out if the parent is too busy or is having difficulty soothing the baby. Even if there isn't a formal arrangement at your company, accepting offers of help from other people in holding or caring for your baby can be very useful—both to give you a few dedicated minutes for a complex work problem or simply to visit the restroom. It also gives you the opportunity to see how other people interact with babies. Many people love playing with and talking to babies for brief periods of time and are likely to welcome the opportunity.

# Integrate Your Child Into the World

Babies can understand and adapt to their surroundings far more than most people realize. If you repeatedly use the same word or phrase to describe a basic concept to your baby, she will quickly start to grasp the meaning behind what you're saying. Babies can (and want to) learn the rules of the world very quickly, even in those early months. For example, tell your baby (when appropriate) that an item is "not for eating" and show her other things to do with the object. After some repetition of this, your baby will relatively quickly learn not to put that item into her mouth. Babies are capable of tremendous understanding and of learning "rules" if they are given appropriate stimulation and guidance, which will make your life as a parent (and your baby's life) far happier and easier as your baby grows older.

Given how physically helpless babies are at birth, sometimes it's hard to remember how powerful their minds are. One perspective I recently heard is to think of your child as a visitor from another planet, with rights, views, and emotions as clear as your own, but who just doesn't yet speak our language. If you can keep in mind that your baby is highly intelligent and capable of profound understanding (which they are) and treat them that way, your child is very likely to live up to that view.

Babies—like older children and adults—want to have their physical needs met, they want to interact with other people, and they want to feel that someone they love and trust is close by. The more assistance you can give your baby in fulfilling these desires, the happier your baby will be, and the more easily you will be able to complete your non-baby-related tasks.

| **3** | Top Ten Tips for A Successful Baby Program |
|-------|---------------------------------------------|
|       | ## Set Clear Rules                          |

# 10

# KEEPING BABIES HAPPY

Using the biologically-based baby care practices described in this book (holding your baby as much as possible and responding immediately to her requests for help, breastfeeding frequently if possible, keeping your baby close during sleep, and giving your baby sufficient social stimulation) will greatly increase the likelihood that your baby will be highly content and will not cry for prolonged periods. However, there are situations in which even babies raised using these methods sometimes cry for long periods or have colic (which is commonly described with the "Rule of 3s"—a baby crying intensely for more than three days a week, for more than three hours, for more than three weeks in a month, without an obviously identifiable medical reason). This chapter is designed to address common causes of crying and colic, and to provide effective resources for parents to identify and solve the reason for their babies' unhappiness.

It can often be useful, particularly as a new parent, to have a list in mind of the most common reasons babies cry. This enables you to go through the list as a routine until you get to better know your baby and are able to more quickly figure out what she needs.  One such checklist could be:

- Hungry
- Wants to nurse/suck even if not hungry
- Wants to be held
- Wants to go to sleep
- Too hot
- Too cold
- Bored
- Overstimulated (needs quiet/calm)
- Pain (hair wrapped around finger or clothing too tight)

Many mothers find that nursing (or letting your baby suck on a pacifier if you're not breastfeeding) is effective at making a baby happy a great majority of the time, so don't hesitate to make the most of this option—frequent breastfeeding is very good for your baby (and will help to build your milk supply).

## The Happiest Baby on the Block

Dr. Harvey Karp's "colic cure" methods, described in his best-selling book *The Happiest Baby on the Block: The New Way to Calm Crying and Help Your Newborn Baby Sleep Longer* (and related materials such as DVDs illustrating the methods), are gaining widespread attention for their effectiveness in calming fussy babies.  Dr. Karp's methods are based on his extensive research into practices in indigenous cultures that often result in rapid contentment for crying babies.  Dr. Karp maintains a detailed website (www.TheHappiestBaby.com) about his research and certifies parent-educators around the country who do one-on-one consultations with parents to teach these methods.

## Dunstan Baby Language System

Priscilla Dunstan (www.DunstanBaby.com) carefully analyzed the sounds made by babies and created a system for determining what basic need a baby has by his specific type of cry. The effectiveness of the Dunstan method has been tested on more than 1,000 babies (and independently assessed by studies) and may be highly useful for parents seeking a more effective way to rapidly determine what their baby needs.

## Physical Misalignment / Baby Chiropractic

Babies can sometimes suffer from pain and discomfort in the early weeks of life as a result of physical trauma during the birth process. A number of parents have had great success with chiropractic care for babies who cry for prolonged periods. Several studies have shown positive results from this option. It is important to find a chiropractor who has experience treating babies—baby chiropractic care is much different from and gentler than that sometimes used in adult care.

## Infant Massage

Infant massage is often an effective way to soothe a colicky baby and to keep your baby happier and calmer in general (and it is also a great way to provide your baby with the gentle touch that is so critical for their proper growth). Infant Massage USA trains parent-educators and provides information on effective techniques. A recommended book on how to massage your baby is *Infant Massage—A Handbook for Loving Parents* by Vimala Schneider McClure.

# Allergies

Undiagnosed allergies can sometimes result in unhappy babies. The most common allergen for babies is dairy products (which might be in formula or transmitted through a breastfeeding mother's milk and can cause a wide range of possible symptoms including wheezing, stuffiness, and eczema), but there are a number of other possible triggers. Along with providing useful information on breastfeeding (as mentioned earlier), www.KellyMom.com also contains clear, accurate information on many parenting topics, including how to analyze whether your baby might have a previously undiagnosed allergy.

# Homeopathics and Other Alternative Treatments

A growing number of parents are trying homeopathic remedies for various ailments, including teething pain and colic. The basic philosophy of homeopathy is extreme dilution of substances that would, in a healthy person, cause the illness that you want to treat. The idea is basically that, by giving the body a minuscule amount of an unwanted substance, the body is triggered to produce its own defenses and thus cure the illness on its own. This is one of those instances where it's hard to believe logically that this concept could work, but alternative remedies like homeopathy are becoming more popular (although the scientific evidence showing their effectiveness is limited).

If you want to try this option or other alternative methods such as herbal remedies, do your research and be selective about the companies from which you purchase products. A reputable company whose products are found in many health food stores is Hylands Homeopathy. Many parents (including our own family) have found their teething tablets to be particularly effective for babies. The risks of side effects from reputable homeopathic products are very remote, particularly compared to many over-the-counter medications.

## Keys for Helping Your Baby

Keep your pediatrician involved with any efforts you may be making to help your baby if she's crying for prolonged periods, but don't be afraid to try a number of different things to see what might help. The most important thing to keep in mind if your baby is crying (while you're trying to discover the reason) is that the best thing you can do for your baby is simply to *be there* for them—hold them, talk to them, sing to them, and just let them know they're not alone.

| 2 | Top Ten Tips for A Successful Baby Program |
|---|---|
|   | Allow Babies Until Mobile |

# 11

# CONCLUSION

Letting parents bring their babies to work is an idea that sounds impractical on the surface. After all, how could a modern, professional company possibly do business with a bunch of babies around? But it turns out that, in an age of computers and automation and a time of globalization and fierce competition, companies who consider babies to be just part of a normal workday may have found a key to success. In today's difficult economy, the real question is, *if it works*, why would a business *not* try a program with such little cost and such extensive rewards?

The success of structured babies-at-work programs reminds us that people have worked with their children by their sides for most of human history. These programs illustrate that, in spite of the perceptions of many in our society, it is not biologically normal for babies to cry for long periods of time and that there are extensive parenting tools available—often literally at our fingertips—for raising socially aware, highly content babies. Most importantly, they prove that millions of today's jobs could successfully be done at the same time we parent our children—with benefits for all of us.

| 1 | Top Ten Tips for A Successful Baby Program |
|---|---|
| | Have a Written Policy |

# 12

# SUGGESTED LINKS

Attachment Parenting International
(www.AttachmentParenting.org)

The Baby Wearer
(www.TheBabyWearer.com)

KellyMom (Breastfeeding and Parenting)
(www.KellyMom.com)

MomsRising
(www.MomsRising.org)

The Natural Child Project
(www.NaturalChild.org)

Sloan Work and Family Research Network
(WFNetwork.bc.edu)

Talaris Institute
(www.Talaris.org)

WFC Resources
(www.WorkFamily.com)

Wears The Baby
(www.WearsTheBaby.com)

Winning Workplaces
(www.WinningWorkplaces.org)

Work and Pump
(www.WorkAndPump.com)

**13**

# SUGGESTED BOOKS

*The Attachment Parenting Book: A Commonsense Guide to
Understanding and Nurturing Your Baby*
   by William Sears, M.D., and Martha Sears

*The Baby Book: Everything You Need to Know About Your Baby
from Birth to Age Two*
   by William Sears, M.D., and Martha Sears

*Birth Without Violence: The Book That Revolutionalized
the Way We Bring Our Children into the World*
   by Frederick Leboyer, M.D.

*The Breastfeeding Book: Everything You Need to Know
About Nursing Your Child from Birth Through Weaning*
   by William Sears, M.D., and Martha Sears

*Einstein Never Used Flash Cards: How Our Children Really Learn—
And Why They Need to Play More and Memorize Less*
   by Kathy Hirsh-Pasek, Ph.D., Roberta Michnick
   Golinkoff, Ph.D., and Diane Eyer, Ph.D.

*The First Idea: How Symbols, Language, And Intelligence Evolved
From Our Primate Ancestors To Modern Humans*
   by Stanley I. Greenspan, M.D., and Stuart G. Shanker, D.Phil.

*The Happiest Baby on the Block: The New Way to Calm Crying
and Help Your Newborn Baby Sleep Longer*
   by Harvey Karp, M.D.

*How to Talk So Kids Will Listen and Listen So Kids Will Talk*
    by Adele Faber and Elaine Mazlish

*The No-Cry Sleep Solution: Gentle Ways to Help Your Baby
Sleep Through the Night*
    by Elizabeth Pantley

*Our Babies, Ourselves: How Biology and Culture Shape
the Way We Parent*
    by Meredith Small, Ph.D.

*The Parent's Guide to Family-Friendly Work: Finding the Balance
Between Employment and Enjoyment*
    by Lori K. Long, Ph.D.

*Raising Our Children, Raising Ourselves: Transforming Parent-child
Relationships from Reaction And Struggle to Freedom, Power And Joy*
    by Naomi Aldort, Ph.D.

*The Science of Parenting*
    by Professor Margot Sunderland

*The Scientist in the Crib: What Early Learning Tells Us
About the Mind*
    by Alison Gopnik, Ph.D., Andrew N. Meltzoff, Ph.D.,
    and Patricia K. Kuhl, Ph.D.

*Sleeping With Your Baby: A Parent's Guide to Cosleeping*
    by James J. McKenna, Ph.D.

*Social Intelligence: The New Science of Human Relationships*
    by Daniel Goleman, Ph.D.

*Working Without Weaning: A Working Mother's Guide
to Breastfeeding*
    by Kirsten Berggren, Ph.D.

# 14

# PARENTING IN THE WORKPLACE INSTITUTE

The largest obstacles to widespread implementation of parenting-at-work programs are (1) lack of awareness of their viability and benefits and (2) lack of knowledge about how to set up an effective program and address potential problems. The Parenting in the Workplace Institute is devoted to overcoming those obstacles through extensive grassroots outreach and media coverage about the viability of babies-at-work programs and programs involving older children, as well as by creating and disseminating "best practices" documentation to enable organizations to easily and inexpensively implement sustainable programs.

The Institute's website currently offers a downloadable fact sheet about babies-at-work programs and a template policy that combines the most effective provisions from organizations with successful programs. We are working on other materials, such as a guide for parents on working with a baby and a summary sheet of the benefits for businesses. The Institute provides direct assistance—including email and telephone support—to organizations and individuals wishing to set up new baby programs as well as to organizations with existing programs that wish to increase the sustainability or effectiveness of their policies.

As we grow, we anticipate providing on-site support to organizations as applicable. We welcome your ideas for furthering our work, would love to hear your stories about parenting in the workplace, and would love to know about any organizations (worldwide) that currently allow parenting in the workplace. Our ever-growing database of companies with active programs can be found on our Baby-Friendly Company List on the Babies in the Workplace site (www.BabiesAtWork.org).

Contact Information:

Parenting in the Workplace Institute
39 Edwards Street
Framingham, MA 01701
(801) 897-8702
carla@babiesatwork.org
www.BabiesAtWork.org
www.ParentingAtWork.org

# ABOUT THE AUTHOR

Carla Moquin lives in Massachusetts, is 31 years old, and is raising two wonderful daughters who are 3 and nearly 7 years of age, respectively. She has a bachelor's degree in psychology from the Pennsylvania State University, a master's-level certification in mediation and facilitation skills from the University of Utah, and was on the Dean's List during her three years of attendance at Concord University School of Law. Ms. Moquin has been researching babies-at-work programs since 2005. She is the founder and president of the Parenting in the Workplace Institute (www.ParentingAtWork.org), based in Framingham, Massachusetts. She maintains the blog Working With Kids (www.WorkingWithKids.org) about integrating children into society. Ms. Moquin has been the spokesperson for the Institute in more than a dozen live and recorded radio and television interviews, as well as for several print articles about babies-at-work programs.

Ms. Moquin conducts ongoing research on baby development and methods for raising babies and children to enable them to be healthy, happy, and to successfully integrate into society. She hopes to spend the rest of her professional life educating and providing resources for sustainable parenting-at-work programs around the world.